D0525154

# The Little Money Book

## by
David Boyle

*To my wonderful cousins, and especially Judith Hodge, for our joint endeavours; and Penelope Newsome, who first introduced me to the possibilities of greening the economy.*

David Boyle is an associate of the New Economics Foundation, and the author of *Funny Money*, *The Tyranny of Numbers*, *The Money Changers* and *Authenticity: Brands, Fakes, Spin and the Lust for Real Life* (HarperCollins/Flamingo).

Written and researched by David Boyle
Published by Fragile Earth Books, an imprint of Alastair Sawday Publishing
Cover design: Caroline King
Overall design concept: Caroline King
Illustrations: ©Zedcor Inc
Cover image: Image Colour Library
Printing: Pims Print Ltd

ISBN 1-901970-51-5

Printed in the UK

The publishers have made every effort to ensure the accuracy of the information in the book at the time
of going to press. However, they cannot accept any responsibility for any loss, injury or inconvenience
resulting from the use of information contained in this guide.

# Contents

# Why publish this book?

*Lurking within the gargantuan machine that is the financial system are some very bizarre, and even astonishing, 'truths'. We, the world's richest countries, demand billions of dollars annually as interest payments on loans made to previous rulers of poor countries. In many cases they were corrupt rulers put there and propped up by 'us'.*

*The following fascinating (and lightly edited) speech to European heads of state – by a representative of South American indigenous communities – is worth every second of your reading time:*

"I, Guaicaipuro Cuatemoc, have come to meet with the participants of this meeting."Here I, descendent of those who have lived in America for 40,000 years, have come to meet with those who met us 500 years ago.

"My brother, the European usurer, asks me to repay a debt of treachery from a Judas I never authorized to put me up for collateral.

"My brother, the European hypocrite, explains to me that all debts must be paid with interest even while he buys and sells human beings and entire countries without their consent.

"I have been discovering these things. I too claim payment and I too claim interest.

"Proven it is, in the archives of native peoples, by paper upon paper, receipt upon receipt, and signature upon signature, that between the years 1503 and 1660 there arrived at San Lucas de Barrameda 185,000 kilos of gold and 16,000,000 kilos of silver from the Americas.

"Those 185,000 kilos of gold and 16,000,000 kilos of silver should be seen as the first of many, many friendly loans from the Americas towards European development. The contrary would be to assume war crimes and not only immediate recompense, but indemnity for damages, pain and suffering.

"Such a fabulous transfer of capital was no less than the beginning of a 'Marshall Tesuma' plan, to guarantee the reconstruction of a barbaric Europe, ruined by wars against (a very civilised) Islam.

"So. To celebrate the Fifth Centennial of the IOU, we can ask: have our European brothers made rational, responsible or even productive use of these amounts so generously advanced by the International Indo-american Fund?

"Sadly, the answer is - 'no'. In their campaigns they squandered it – in the battles of Lepanto, in invincible armadas, in third reichs, in every form of mutual extermination.

They have been unable, despite a 500-year moratorium, to repay the principal and interest, let alone to live free of the further dividends, the raw materials and cheap energy exported and continually provided to them by all the 'third world'.

This deplorable vista corroborates Milton Friedman's view that a subsidised economy can never function and obliges us, for their own good, to demand payment of the principal and interest that we have waited so generously for all these centuries to reclaim. Let it be clear that we do not stoop to charging the villainous leech rates of 20% and up to 30% that our European brothers charge the peoples of the third world. We merely require the return of the precious metals advanced, plus the modest accumulated interest of 10% for a period of 300 years with a 200 year period of grace.

On this basis, and applying the European formula for compound interest, we advise our 'discoverers' that they owe us, as initial payment on the debt, a mass of 185,000 kilos of gold and 16,000,000 kilos of silver. As for the interest, we are owed 440,000,000,000,000,000 kilos of gold and 38,000,000,000,000,000,000 kilos of silver (or 1% of the mass of the moon). At the rates of mid 2002 that equates to a total of US$391,000,000,000,000,000,000 or 391 million million million dollars.

To infer that Europe, in half a millennium, has not been able to generate sufficient wealth to pay off this modest interest, would be to admit the abject failure of its financial system and the demented irrationality of the premises of capitalism.

Such metaphysical questions, however, do not disturb us Indo-americans.

But, what if we were to require the signing of a Letter of Intent to discipline the indebted peoples of the Old World, and to oblige them to fulfill their obligations by means of rapid privatisations and fiscal restraint, as the first step in payment of this historic debt...

Guaicaipuro Cuatemoc

# Introduction

*"There is no wealth but life. Life, including all its powers of love, of joy, and of admiration. That country is the richest which nourishes the greatest number of noble and happy human beings; that man is richest who, having perfected the functions of his own life to the utmost, has also the widest helpful influence, both personal, and by means of his possessions, over the lives of others."*
John Ruskin, *Unto This Last*

From the poorest to the most wealthy, we worry about money. We worry about our bank balance, our shares, our retirement, our bills. We imagine that a little extra could solve all our problems yet, bizarrely, it is in the richest country in the world – the USA – where people worry most and are, apparently, most depressed.

Worse, when we grapple with our finances, we are confronted with a fearsome cadre of financial advisers some of whom seem prepared to tell us almost anything to get their hands on our cash, and who insist on using a peculiar and impenetrable jargon. What are endowments, negative equity, derivatives, hedge funds and all the rest of them? They'd like you to feel that you couldn't possibly find out without them.

Perhaps it isn't surprising that many of us bolt the door and – like Sir Alec Douglas-Home when he was Chancellor of the Exchequer – put our heads in a hot towel and balance our budgets using matchsticks. Or failing that, keep our fingers crossed and hope for the best.

It's a strange peculiarity of modern life that we struggle with money as much as we do. We live in the richest societies in the history of humanity, yet we spend more time than ever worrying about money. We worry about it partly because we never seem to have enough, and partly because we are constantly encouraged to do so. Advertising – and articles in the personal finance pages of Sunday newspapers – urge us to be a little more nervous about our house insurance, our car insurance, our mortgages, credit card APR, unsecured loans, unit trusts, Personal Equity Plans, pensions and burial cover.

Most of us don't understand the arcane system by which the total in our pension is worked out every year or the actuarial tables by which our life insurance is calculated. And we haven't really got time to master it either, along with all the other things we have to do with our lives – but we don't wholly trust anybody else to do it either.

Yet however much, in response, we leave the final demands unopened and push money to the backs of our minds, we are aware of it bubbling away like a volcano – the strange, terrifyingly powerful, barely-understood machine that seems to drive the whole world.

We are aware of its contradictions and paradoxes. On the one hand, of course, money is an expression of the underlying wealth of the earth. It has real and powerful effects – sometimes devastating – on people and planet alike. On the other hand, it is intangible, flowing through the world's computer screens as electronic blips at the rate of $2,000 billion a day, trading in ethereal products that – like oil futures or the future value of the dollar over the yen – have no real existence at all, in quantities that the earth could never produce anyway.

We can't see money. It slips through every definition. Yet sometimes it is the most powerful force in the world, and can so take control of people's minds that real aspects of life – like trees, people, rivers or species – get ignored and then swept from the collective memory.

So next time you puzzle over your bank statement, or wonder whether you were right – urged on by neighbours and financial advisers alike – to take out that endowment mortgage in the late 1980s (as I did), remember that you're not alone. Money and the complex system that makes it work is a man-made product that we invented, and though – like Frankenstein – it has us all in its grip, whether through fascination, complexity or sheer intractability, we should be able to change the rules by which it works.

If we feel we can comment on its inner workings again, or invent our own, and find whole new ways that money can work *for* people rather than setting them against each other – we might be able, between us, to claw back some kind of control.

So this Little Book is intended to redress the balance of power a little. It isn't like the glossy financial guides pressed into our hands by sales representative from our banks or insurance companies, which will tell us a small amount about how they can provide us with yet more products that come as statements every quarter. Nor is it anything like an economics textbook, full of graphs that ward off those who have not been admitted into the narrow world of the economics cognoscenti. But it will tell you where money comes from, what it means, and what it's doing to the planet – and what we might be able to do about it.

This is a financial guide that may not tell you how to invest your money – though it might give you some ideas – but it will tell you all the things you wanted to know that made your bank manager look a little blank when you asked.

It will also brief you for the emerging debate about money – not just how can we get more of it, but what is it doing to us, aren't there better ways of creating it, couldn't we do without it for a while? And it will tell you the truth that politicians and brokers alike prefer not to think about too much – the way they have lost control of a gigantic financial system that could enrich or impoverish us all in seconds if it chose to do so.

In short, this Little Book could make you look at everything from your bank statements to the coins in your pocket in a whole new way. It could even change your life.

*David Boyle*

Section I

# Metal Money

Money can be anything you like. The trouble is that we all live in a world that confuses money with real wealth, that muddles money and what you have in the bank with eternal human values. So it is hardly surprising that we are all getting a bit obsessed with money.

# What is money?

## and where has it come from?

For something we all use so much of, and think about as much as we do, money is extraordinarily elusive. Nobody quite agrees what it is or even sometimes what it's for.

At the end of the spectrum, it can be shells from the beach which are used as money in parts of Polynesia. It can be 12-foot round blocks of stone, used as money in the Caroline Islands – unlikely to be stolen out of your handbag but less than useful as small change. Or, if you're in Wall Street, money can be screeds and screeds of digital information, unrelated to any product in the real world.

It isn't that one is real and the other isn't. Both are profoundly real and relate to the different functions that money plays. According to the economists there are three of these: as a store of value (like the stones), as a standard of value (which everyone can understand) and as a medium of exchange (like the shells – they need have no value in themselves, but help you exchange at an exact price).

Money can be anything – like cigarettes – which helps you account for what you need to buy. It can be something valuable, like coins. It can be something scarce like gold, with intrinsic value. It can be something sophisticated and elastic like shares or copper futures. It can be something that can be accidentally deleted by your bank just because someone sits on the keyboard (this happens surprisingly often). And sometimes it can be a bit of all of these, like the gold that the Spanish

> *"Money is human happiness in the abstract; and so, the man who is no longer capable of enjoying such happiness in the concrete sets his whole heart on money."*
> Arthur Schopenhauer

'conquistadores' found in Latin America, extracted from the Incas and shipped back to Europe. Almost anything can be used as money.

The trouble for us is that money is a bit of all those things. It is coins and it is debt. It is credit card plastic and it is infinite bytes and bytes and bytes in cyberspace – the place where banks actually keep our deposits.

Except that for some of us, money is a good deal more elastic than it is for others. While the poorest people in the world make do with the equivalent of a few pence a day, the 'masters of the universe' in Wall Street and the City of London – as Tom Wolfe called them in The Bonfire of the Vanities – have a money system that is almost infinitely elastic. When the rogue financier Robert Maxwell fell off his yacht in the Bay of Biscay in 1991, he had stretched his money so much that he owed twice as much as Zimbabwe. Of all the great injustices of the money system, that is the heart of it. For some people money is stretchy, insubstantial and infinite, for others it is horribly concrete. Some people make and remake the rules; some people die by them.

But where does it come from in the first place? There is a popular misconception that the wealth of the world is underpinned by great bars of gold in the vaults of the Bank of England, the Federal Reserve and Fort Knox. Not any more it isn't.

There is still gold in the vaults, and it is still shifted from cage to cage – each one assigned to a different world government – rather than shipped round the world. But that's an historic anomaly and a simple way of storing some of the nation's reserves. Central banks actually spent most of the 1990s trying to sell off their gold reserves surreptitiously without lowering the world gold price. (They failed.)

Actually, the pound hasn't been backed by gold since 1931 at the height of the Great Depression, and the final link between money and gold was broken in 1971 when Richard Nixon finally ended the pretence that the US dollar had gold backing. Now if you read the 'promise to pay the bearer on demand' message on your £5 note and you take it to the Bank of England, they will simply give you another £5 note in return.

Of course there are coins, but these are made of cupro-nickel and are no longer worth anything like the 10p or 50p on the front. The total value of notes and coins produced by the Royal Mint and issued into circulation by the Bank of England and its equivalents is only a tiny 3% of all the money in circulation.

Where does all the rest come from? Well, astonishingly, nobody agrees. But most people seem to accept that it is lent into existence by the commercial banks. When you stash money in the bank, they must keep around 8% of that loan on deposit – in case there's a run on the bank – but all the rest is lent out again many times over. In other words, most of our mortgages and bank loans are created as if by magic by a stroke of the pen.

And one day it will have to be paid back, plus interest to the bank, when it can be used as the 8% backing for yet more loans. And so it goes on. It's a magical money-making system that is surprisingly little commented on, limited these days by only two things: the regulations of the Bank for International Settlements in Basle, and fear of having to pay it back if the loan fails – and a good 10% usually do fail.

That's the strange truth behind modern money. We don't mine it, we don't find it on a beach, it bears no relation to anything real, but still some people have vast amounts of it and some people have none at all. And we hardly ever talk about it.

John Kenneth Galbraith
*Money: Whence it came, where it went*
Penguin, 1975    ISBN 0140234799

# Origins of money
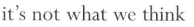

## it's not what we think

*"The worse thing is not giving presents. We give what we have. That is the way we live together."*
Kalahari bushman, quoted in William Bloom's
*Money, Heart and Mind*

There are so many myths about money, and the myths lie behind so much of what we are told about economics, that it would take more than a Little Book to outline them all. But the first, and the most insidious myth is about its origin.

We are constantly told by economists and politicians that money began as a way of facilitating trade. We are told that it developed because barter was inefficient and that, for this reason, the drive towards individual wealth and competition that seems at the heart of economics is also at the heart of all of us. Or that money is just an expression of our inner drive to compete with each other in business. This is just not true; neither greed nor inefficiencies

'drove' the growth of money. Of course barter had its inefficiencies. You have to want what the other person's got, and life doesn't always work like that. The barter schemes that allow some societies to get by without enough cash – like Russia during the 1990s – are fiendishly complicated and devilishly inconvenient (see p 162). But that wasn't why money began.

Most anthropologists agree that money started as a form of ritual gift – in the form of something you gave the next door tribe when you met, or gave the father of the woman you were going to marry, or gave to God at the temple. The word 'pay' comes from the Latin 'pacare', which means to pacify, appease, or make peace with. Money began as a way to make peace.

Take, for example, the meeting between Solomon and the Queen of Sheba around 950 BC. "Extravagant ostentation, the attempt to outdo each other in the splendour of the exchanges, and above all, the obligations of reciprocity were just as typical in this celebrated encounter, though at a fittingly princely level, as with the more mundane types of barter in other parts of the world," says Glyn Davies, author of The History of Money.

In fact, the ornamental metallic objects known as 'manillas' in West Africa were used as money as recently as 1949. Some ceremonies in the Pacific still use special whale's teeth or edible rats as ritual gifts of money; the origins of money are still there to see if you are sharp enough. But they have always been regarded with a peculiar horror by modern economists, and officials have even tried to stamp the whole idea out. Canadian authorities outlawed native American 'potlatch' ceremonies – the mixture between social, ceremonial, ritual and barter that were the heart of their societies – between 1884 and 1951.

What does this mean? It means that economics wasn't originally about savage people competing over scarce resources, using money to do each other down. It was about mutual recognition and facilitating human relationships. It's important to remember this now that money's secondary function is to replace human relationships with monetary ones. When things are sold rather than given, when old people live in nursing homes rather than with their children, relationships get driven out by money.

"This is to say that people do not work and create the economy because they want to support the economy," says the writer William Bloom. "They create and relate – and this, in turn, creates the economy." So don't be taken in by economics. We created the economy around us, and if we want to change it, we can do just that.

*"The customs of the Lydians differ little from those of the Graecians, except that they prostitute their females."*

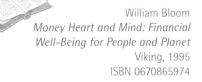

William Bloom
*Money Heart and Mind: Financial Well-Being for People and Planet*
Viking, 1995
ISBN 0670865974

# Gold

## The barbarous relic

Herodotus on the inventors of modern money

Herodotus was talking about the first coins, invented in the seventh century BC by the Lydians, living in what is now Turkey. Within a century or so the idea had spread to Greece and North Africa. Even in China, they were making metal versions of the tools and shells that had been used as money before to serve as coinage.

The trouble was, as Herodotus points out, that the shift to metal coins wasn't very honourable – more to do with prostitution than the beginnings of a great trading empire: the Lydians were actually the first pimps. But it meant that people could be extremely precise about price and debt in a way they couldn't before. Unfortunately, coins confused people about the nature of wealth. The money they were using began as a token of wealth, but soon it became all important; people believed that gold or silver was the wealth itself, and soon humanity had become caught up in its now-familiar muddle about money. Whatever they know in their hearts, they often act as if:

• Metal is wealth, rather than a manifestation of the intrinsic wealth we carry around inside us as human beings.

• The total amount of wealth is somehow limited to how much gold there is in the world – so that there isn't nearly enough money to go around.

• Only gold – or things that can get you gold – are important.

• The things that are valuable in terms of money (houses, burger franchises, diamond rings) are *really* valuable compared to things that money can't give value to such as orphans, nurses, love.

Those errors have led to the most appalling human mistakes. The conquistadors who followed Christopher Columbus to the New World in 1492 set about cutting the gold jewellery off the locals and hauling it back across the Atlantic in such quantities that it caused disastrous inflation for well over a century.

We make the same mistakes today when economists persuade us that money is all that's important and only things that can be reduced to money – trees after they've been cut down, great works of nature as tourist resorts – are worth measuring or protecting. "Industrial humanity is behaving like King Midas," wrote Paul Ekins in *Wealth Beyond Measure*. "He turned his daughter into gold before he realised the limitations of his own conception of wealth."

Gold may be a 'barbarous relic', according to the great economist John Maynard Keynes, but in times of uncertainty we still hanker for it. Most currencies haven't been based on gold since 1931. But, quite reasonably, we want our money to be based on something real – rather than the bytes and bytes of information about debt that it is these days.

The trouble is that there isn't nearly enough gold in the world to satisfy our needs for a medium of exchange – just enough for the very rich. Since Columbus returned from his first voyage, about 1.5 billion ounces of refined gold have come out of the ground, only enough to fill a couple of small semi-detached houses.

You can see them in bars underneath the Bank of England or the Federal Reserve of New York, each one worth the same as a London flat. It's exclusive and scarce – not enough to provide money for most of us.

Glyn Davies
*A History of Money from the Earliest Times to the Present Day*
University of Wales Press, 2002
ISBN 0708317170

# Inflation

## Columbus and original sin

*"Wall Street, in theory, is the centre of the financial system which provides for the capital needs of the nation. But Wall Street is in fact a speculation centre organised for the purpose of enabling a self-selected minority of men of boundless greed and ambition to become millionaires and billionaires. Whatever Wall Street does to provide for the capital needs of the nation is incidental to, and misshaped and distorted, by what it in fact is."*

Ralph Borsodi, pioneer green campaigner

The galleons of gold that Columbus brought home caused ruinous inflation. Suddenly there was too much money flooding into the continent, chasing exactly the same number of

goods – and that's what causes prices to rise. A century after Columbus, there was eight times more money in circulation in Europe, and the reserves of the Spanish and Ottoman empires had been devastated. Its own success had brought down the Spanish empire.

In the last few decades in Britain, during which we have had to live with rapidly rising prices, anyone might be forgiven for thinking that inflation was something caused by greedy unions and high wages. We might be forgiven for swallowing the idea that we have to cure it by squeezing the economy dry of money – a process known as monetarism.

But these are misconceptions. Actually, we need money to live. If you squeeze the supply of money, the first people to suffer are the poorest. And without money, we all die – "like a peregrination in the catacombs," said Keynes, "with a guttering candle." Economics has now reached the stage of bleeding the patient.

That's not the reason prices go up. More money has to be balanced by more goods and services. If money is created for speculation – and at least 97% of the money changing hands is now for short-term speculation – then it's going to be inflationary. And even worse, if banks create money just with a stroke of a pen by lending it as a debt – with interest attached – then that's inflationary too (see p 89).

If the amount of money in circulation keeps growing at the rate it has in the UK in the past 30 years, we will have £14,000 billion in the economy in 2022; now it is somewhere around £700 billion. Yet the banks only mint a tiny proportion of that: all the rest is lent into existence by banks and building societies.

All this money is chasing almost the same number of goods, but most of it is sloshing through the electronic markets as speculation.

So the prices of luxuries are rising fast: we have had serious inflation in house prices for three decades. The prices of other things are not rising, primarily because financial authorities make sure very little of this bonanza trickles down to ordinary people. For them the squeeze remains in force.

According to the campaigners of the mid-20th century, inflation was theft. The government undermined the value of our money by printing too much of it. True – but the opposite is also true: by squeezing the money out of the real economy, or goods and people, they are also squeezing out the lives of ordinary people.

*Money in circulation in UK*
*1971        £31 billion*
*1996        £665 billion (up 2,145%)*

Ralph Borsodi
*Inflation and the Coming*
*Keynesian Catastrophe*
E. F. Schumacher Society, 1979

# Usury

## The great debate

Muslims have a concept they call zakat, which means that everyone needs to pay what they can afford to help the community. It's a tradition and it supports the Islamic idea that nobody should be allowed to starve. Rich people should not press their debts too far and, when necessary, should forgive them.

But then this doesn't just apply to Muslims. Strip away some of the old stories about sheep or goats, and all the great world religions have similar economic ideas at their heart: letting people rest every seven days, letting the land lie fallow and forgiving debts every seven years. And they all condemn what they call 'usury'.

Usury has been at the heart of Christian debate for the past 2,000 years – and Islam still believes that the charging of all interest is wrong (see p

*"Those who swallow usury cannot rise except as one whom Satan has prostrate by his touch."*
The Koran

85). In the Middle Ages, though, Christian theology began to accept interest, as long as it was fair. But pursuing people for generations because of unpaid debts, which were rising all the time because of compound interest, was still considered seriously wrong.

Islamic banks are now some of the fastest growing sectors of financial services (see p 85), refusing to charge interest but sharing ownership instead. The idea is to make sure that money is productive and doesn't just breed all by itself. But however you define it, usury remains with us.

On the small scale there are the money-lenders and loan sharks who prey on the poorest in society. While typical mainstream interest on credit cards or personal loans ranges between 5 and 17% APR (annual percentage rate), loans offered on the doorstep of a council flat – for people too poor to borrow money from banks – can amass an inclusive APR of more than 1,000%. Recent research showed one loan shark charging 1,834%, and even 5,000% has been known.

All over Britain you can see people queuing up outside the Benefits Office with their loan shark, who has taken their benefits book as 'security', only to lend it back so they can hand over their dole money to pay the interest on their loan.

On a larger scale is the scandal of debts foisted on impoverished people by their own governments and the Western banks which they can never repay. This has led to some bizarre peculiarities (see p 89), including:

- Everyone in the Third World owes an average of £250 to the West – more than a year's wage for most of them.

- Africa spends four times as much on debt repayment as it does on health.

- The commission paid on the ruinous £55 billion 'mega-swap' loan to Argentina in 2000 – which brought about its financial crisis, and involved 'usurious' interest rates – was £150 million, to bankers in London, New York and Buenos Aires.

- Europe used to sell a fifth of its exports to the Third World, especially Africa: now they are too poor to buy more than a tenth.

Most people accept that money has to be paid for somehow when it is lent, but dislike anyone taking advantage of the desperate or needy. When Coca-Cola developed vending machines that would charge more in hot weather, this was widely denounced. The old condemnation of usury still provided moral guidance.

Henry Palmer and Pat Conaty
*Profiting from Poverty*
New Economics Foundation, 2003
ISBN 1 899407 61 8

# The World Bank and the IMF

## International expense accounts

*"Future students of history will be shocked and angered by the fact that in 1945 the same monetary system that had driven the world to despair and disaster [in the Great Depression], and had almost destroyed the civilisation it was supposed to stand for, was revived on a much wider scope."*
Jacques Rueff

The world's top economists made their way across the submarine-infested Atlantic in 1944 for the Bretton Woods conference in New Hampshire, to plan the future financial shape of the world.

It was a hopeful moment. But the British plan, devised by the great economist John Maynard Keynes, was thrown out. He proposed a financial system underpinned by a global currency based on real goods. Instead, the American plan was put in its place. The main legacy of those heady days has been the International Monetary Fund and the World Bank – the first one as a lender of last resort for the world, and the second about reducing poverty to create new markets for the developed world.

Both have remained shadowy, secretive institutions ever since; even the IMF budget is secret. Both could become anachronisms compared with the vast money flows that shoot across the globe 24 hours a day. During the 1998 Asian currency crisis, a desperate finance minister whose currency had come under sudden attack in the world markets called the IMF for advice. But it was after 5pm Washington time and the IMF officials had gone home. The security guard told him he would have to make up his own mind.

Meanwhile, the IMF and World Bank have included among its most grateful clients some of the most unpleasant Third World dictators, including Mobutu, Moi, Samuel Doe, the Argentine junta, Marcos and Pinochet – all regarded as useful to the USA in the Cold War. Of the $26 billion of foreign aid flowing to the Philippine government under his regime, Ferdinand Marcos managed to salt away $10 billion into secret foreign accounts.

Worse, the whole of the $4.4 billion bailout to Russia in 1998 disappeared within days, siphoned out of the economy through secret offshore bank accounts in Cyprus.

Then there have been the 'structural adjustment' programmes enforced on poor countries by the IMF before they would agree to a loan, including swathing cuts in welfare, education, health and environmental programmes. They have also been accused of caring more about the banks than about the poor counties. The £41 billion loan to Brazil in 1999 had more to do with saving the necks of the big US lenders like Citibank, to whom the money went in interest payments.

Structural adjustment also meant that poorer countries should shift resources from growing food for themselves towards cash crops – or anything that could earn the foreign currency they needed to pay the interest on their debts. That's why:

- Costa Rica sold its entire genetic heritage to a US pharmaceutical company for £10 million.
- The IMF pressed Guyana to encourage so much mining and oil that, by 1998, they had sold permits covering 10% of the country, destroying rivers and forests alike.
- IMF programmes in Tanzania led to the loss of 40% of its forests between 1980 and 1993.
- As many as 40% of Bolivia's workforce has to depend on the drugs trade for a living.
- Brazil's environmental programmes were cut by two-thirds to meet the fiscal targets set by the IMF. Their advice to Argentina during the 1990s resulted in the complete collapse of the economy in 2002 (since 1994, Argentina's government deficits were caused entirely by the rising interest on foreign loans).

As for the World Bank, its fatal fascination for big corporations and wasteful projects, big development plans and big bureaucracies has been at the expense of the people who lived in the places they were claiming to help. It even boasted to the US Congress that for every dollar the USA gives the World Bank, $3 comes straight back to American corporations to build roads or dams or other big structures.

Since 1948, the World Bank has financed large dam projects that have forced about 10 million people off their homes and lands. The Bank's 1994 'Resettlement and Development' review admitted that the vast majority of those evicted never got back their previous incomes, and never got any benefits from the dams.

Ironically, the IMF announced in 1999 that it was changing the name of its structural adjustment office to the Poverty Reduction and Growth Facility (PRGF) – precisely what it isn't.

**So what should we do?**

- Reform both institutions to make them more democratic and open.
- Re-galvanise efforts to cancel unsustainable debt.
- Shift the focus from big infrastructure loans to small loans to small entrepreneurs.
- End the tyranny of structural adjustment programmes.
- Help countries avoid borrowing by learning how to create the money they need themselves, and to pay off their debts in their own currencies.

| Share of votes at the IMF | | Proportion of world population |
|---|---|---|
| USA | 18% | 4.3% |
| India | 1.9% | 17% |

Graham Hancock
*The Lords of Poverty*
Macmillan, 1989
ISBN 0333439627

# Big currencies and the euro

## Still dreaming of gold

The great psychologist Carl Jung believed that the Governor of the Bank of England, who presided over the Great Depression, was probably insane. He was, indeed obsessed with gold.

It was said that Governor Montagu Norman crossed the Atlantic in disguise as a 'Mr Skinner' in 1929, for a secret meeting with US monetary officials and to introduce a short monetary shock to force the US back on the gold standard. Instead it produced the depression.

> "'Really,' said the Scarecrow. 'You ought to be ashamed of yourself for being such a humbug.' "
> Frank Baum, *The Wonderful Wizard of Oz*, a coded diatribe against the gold standard and too little money

It's a wonderful conspiracy theory, and there's no doubt that trying to go back to fix the pound to the value of gold – a great imperial dream of money being firm and Victorian - was a disaster. British ministers had such an inflated idea of

their own value – and that of their nation – that they then fixed the pound's value far too high. So nobody could afford British goods and factories closed.

And every time the factories closed, they cut back on public spending a little more. The result was a kind of death, the sort you get when, without money, people with time and skills can't connect with the people who want their work.

When he put the pound back on the gold standard in 1925, Winston Churchill painted a romantic picture of international currencies which "vary together, like ships in harbour whose gangways are joined and who rise and fall together with the tide". It sounds a little like the

euro. The euro is another dream that currencies should all be the same: it's the great imperial dream of gold again – of standardising money.

The trouble is, when you standardise money, you standardise people – and that's a kind of lie. And when you tell lies in economics, eventually things fall apart. In the 1990s, bankers dreamed of giant global currencies – Latin American countries enthusiastically linked their currencies to the dollar. But when the Argentinian peso collapsed as a result, they thought again.

Linking the peso to the US dollar gave them stability, but it was a stability that impoverished them – because the dollar is geared to a very different economy. And that's the problem at the heart of the euro: single currencies tend to favour the rich and impoverish the poor.

They do so because changing the value of their currency, and varying their interest rate, is the way that disadvantaged places are able to make their goods more affordable. When you prevent them from doing that, you trap whole cities and regions. They can't trade their way out.

Even in Britain – where the manufacturing north is so very different from the City of London – a single currency means that the rich get even richer, because everybody isn't the same. That doesn't mean there is anything wrong with the euro in itself, but as a single currency it's just another dream of gold, and that doesn't work for everyone.

So what is the solution? To have complementary currencies that can provide feedback for regions, cities and communities – not instead of the pound or euro, but as well as them (see p 164)? Already the euro is accepted by big retailers across the UK, so the multi-currency world is already beginning to come about.

Jane Jacobs
*Cities and the Wealth of Nations: principles of economic life*
Penguin, 1986
ISBN 0394729110

# Money innovators I

## Adam Smith and free trade

*"People of the same trade seldom meet together even for merriment and diversion, but the conversation ends in a conspiracy against the public or some contrivance to raise prices."*
Adam Smith, *The Wealth of Nations*

Adam Smith was the son of the controller of the customs at Kirkcaldy in Scotland. The exact date of his birth is unknown, but he was one of the great generation of libertarians and practical philosophers that also gave us David Hume and Benjamin Franklin. He is also known as the father of 'free trade', thanks to his book The Wealth of Nations and the idea – which he actually only mentioned once – of the 'invisible hand' of the market.

Smith was actually a moral philosopher, so don't believe it when modern apologists for the mega-rich corporations tell you that somehow business is a uniquely amoral world where all that counts is profit and returns to shareholders. In Adam Smith's philosophy, it was embedded in morality.

Nor would they find much support from Adam Smith for the concentration of economic power, for mergers or acquisitions. Free trade for Smith wasn't about refusing to limit the power of those who were already powerful – quite the reverse. Modern corporations, two of which control half of all the grain imports into the USA, would have horrified him. That's not free trade at all under his definition.

Nor is it what the original English campaigners for free trade in the Victorian Liberal Party meant either. For John Bright and Richard Cobden, campaigning for free trade was a natural extension to campaigning against slavery. It meant the right of free and equal businesses to trade with each other without the state interfering. They never meant the right of the rich and powerful to ride roughshod over the powerless.

But it's worse than that. Modern apologists for large corporations have a horror of independent business or anything they don't control. The natural world, for example, is abundant and diverse and it keeps people free: the mega-corporations are doing what they can to licence it, restrict it and force people to trade – and if they can't do that, destroy it with genetically-engineered organisms. Nor is this anything new: imperial governors in Africa, suspicious of self-sufficiency, used to force locals to grow cash crops by taxing them in imperial currency.

Free trade has to be a free choice. That's why we need to celebrate the continued survival of natural diversity. For example:

• In Java, small farmers cultivate 607 species in their home gardens.

• In sub-Saharan Africa, women cultivate as many as 120 different plants in the spaces left alongside the cash crops, and this is the main source of household food security.

• A single home garden in Thailand has more than 230 species, and African home gardens have more than 60 species of tree.

• Rural families in the Congo eat products from more than 50 different species of tree.

• A study in eastern Nigeria found that home gardens occupying only 2% of a household's farmland accounted for half the farm's total output.

• Home gardens in Indonesia are estimated to provide more than 20% of household income and 40% of domestic food supplies.

Research done by the UN has shown that small biodiverse farms can produce thousands of times more food than large, industrial monocultures.

Global corporations don't like this and can't recognise it, says the biodiversity campaigner

Vandana Shiva: "Global consultants fail to see the 99% of food processing done by women at household level [in India], or by small cottage industry, because it is not controlled by global agribusiness; 99% of India's agro-processing has been intentionally kept at the household level. Now, under the pressure of globalisation, things are changing. Pseudo hygiene laws that shut down the food economy based on small-scale local processing under community control are part of the arsenal used by global agribusiness for establishing market monopolies through force and coercion, not competition."

That's not free trade, that's compulsory trade. And Adam Smith certainly wouldn't have recognised it as moral.

---

**Free Trade in 2003**
President George W Bush's promised total aid package to Africa is $25 billion. Africa needs it, because their farm exports cannot compete with America's. Why not? Perhaps because the US government gives $20 billion in subsidies to its farmers - every year.

David C. Korten
*When Corporations Ruled the World*
Kumarian Press, 1995
ISBN 1887208046

# Money innovators 2

## Keynes and what to do if money stops working

The Wall Street Crash of 1929 heralded a worldwide economic disaster (see p 125); even the two greatest economists in the world, John Maynard Keynes and Irving Fisher, lost a great deal of money. The world then collapsed into the misery of the Great Depression – the extraordinary effect of fear on economics – by cutting back and cutting back. Keynes' solution, scribbling away in his study in Cambridge, was to unbalance the government's budget, borrow money and spend it. "It is often said by wiseacres that we cannot spend more than we earn," wrote Keynes in a letter to the Manchester Guardian in 1932. "That is, of course, true enough of the individual, but it is exceedingly misleading if it is applied to the community as a whole."

*"For what we have spent on the dole in England since the war we could have made our cities the greatest works of man in the world... money thus spent... would make unnecessary any dole."*
John Maynard Keynes,
*National Self-Sufficiency, 1933*

Politicians and economists urged people to sacrifice themselves and cut back. But encouraging people to save doesn't make anybody rich, Keynes said. If we saved everything and spent nothing, we'd all die. We are healthy children, he urged, so we should spend. Money was about life.

"Over against us, standing in the path, there is nothing but a few old gentlemen tightly buttoned-up in their frock coats, who only need to be treated with a little friendly disrespect and bowled over like ninepins," Keynes said. "Quite likely, they will enjoy it themselves, once they have got over the shock."

Keynesian economics meant their governments could rescue dying economies, and President Roosevelt learned the lesson with the New Deal in the USA. Keynes, however, exhausted himself negotiating Britain's enormous debt and designing the post-war financial world. He died at the early age of 62. His ideas ran out of steam, because:

• *Statistics* Keynesianism was taken over by econometricians and technocrats: Keynes was always sceptical of using too many statistics in economics through he also invented GNP. Like Adam Smith, he saw economic problems as moral crises.

• *Governments* Governments lost the ability to predict spending, especially during the self-delusory years of the Vietnam War. The result: serious inflation.

• *Keynes himself* In the long run we are dead, said Keynes about what happens when you borrow and spend. But those of us who were alive needed more advice.

• *Margaret Thatcher* She abolished exchange controls in 1979, as a way to force governments around the world to borrow and spend less. Now if you borrow too much, the currency dealers of the world will send the value of your currency suddenly and catastrophically through the floor. (This doesn't yet apply to the Americans; see p 92.)

But Keynesianism isn't dead. His spirit lives on, if only the conviction that human beings can have some control over the money system and that economics is about morality too. When governments only worry about inflation – and are blind to the dangers of Depression and fear – we may need to recover his lost skills. Deflation is back – at work in the Japanese economy – and the world economy is under threat again.

Paul Strathern
*A Brief History of Economic Genius*
Texere, 2002
ISBN 1587991284

Section II

# Money information

Money used to be something you could touch
and see. It is increasingly disembodied, abstract
and unreal – stretchable for the rich and concrete
for the poor – and it is in danger of driving out the
real world altogether.

# Paper tigers

## The growth of funny money and the start of banking

*"The Currency as we manage it is a wonderful machine. It performs an office when we issue it; it pays and clothes Troops, and provides Victuals and Ammunition; and when we are obliged to issue a Quantity excessive, it pays itself off by Depreciation."*

Benjamin Franklin, who printed many of the notes himself

These days, paper money is actually made of polypropylene, which is eventually recycled and turned into plastic wheelbarrows. It sounds mundane, but there was a time when paper money was the wonder of the world.

Money that isn't worth anything in itself, but stood in for the real stuff, was partly convenience (China), partly a brilliant scheme to add to the world's wealth (France), and partly a revolutionary act (America). It was also a kind of Pandora's Box, which we can never close – and probably wouldn't want to – but which brought with it inflation, staggering wealth and many of the other nightmares and tragedies of modern money.

It was simple under Kubla Khan, as Marco Polo discovered in the 1270s, because he could simply say what the paper was worth and execute anybody who disagreed with him. But when the Stockholm pioneer Johan Palmstruch printed notes in the 17th century, he was condemned to death for causing inflation.

When a Scottish adventurer called John Law escaped to Paris in 1716, on the run from killing a man in a duel in London, his paper money –

based on the value of land¥ in Mississippi – made him briefly the richest man in the world (see p 123). When he turned the whole of France's national debt into paper money, the bubble caused a terrifying collapse in value when the whole edifice collapsed, and he had to flee Paris with his life. The incident paved the way for the French Revolution, three generations later.

Lenin said that the best way to destroy the capitalist system was to debauch the currency. "Lenin was certainly right," wrote Keynes a few decades later. "There is no subtler, no surer way of overturning the existing basis of society."

The truth was that the Pandora's box had already been opened by the first bankers, who were often goldsmiths. They would make loans or advances in the form of money orders or promissory notes, knowing that they had enough gold to underwrite the debt. But it didn't take long for them to realise that they could lend more than the value of the gold they had on deposit, because people very rarely asked for it back. In fact, if they were sensible they could lend out up to ten times what they had on deposit – and let it circulate as money.

Such guile didn't always work: the English king Edward III borrowed a vast sum to pay for the Hundred Years War, and then simply declared himself bankrupt. His Italian bankers collapsed. But usually banks could lend out paper money, now just blips of information, worth many times more than anything they have on deposit. So; they actually create the money by lending it; it then exists, and they earn interest on it.

This is a process known as 'fractional reserve banking', and it lies behind the creation of nearly 97% of the money in circulation today (see p 16). But anyone who has seen a 'run' on the bank, such as in the film It's a Wonderful Life – when everyone panics and asks for their money back – can see the risks we run when such a high proportion of our money is created in this way. The over-indebted Japanese banking system teeters on the edge of calling in all their loans and dragging the world into the worst economic crisis for half a century. These are more dangerous times than bankers would like us to believe.

James Buchan
*Frozen Desire*
Picador, 1997
ISBN 0330369318

# Central banks

## The old lady of Threadneedle Street

There's something about central banks – by nature centralised, arcane and secretive places – that invites conspiracy theories, especially in the USA. It is said, for example, by fundamentalists and strange right-wing sects that they were set up to control the world's money, and create their own. If this was ever true, it isn't true now – the truth is much more worrying.

It is true that the US Federal Reserve was set up in 1913 as a private company, and it still is one – though its governors are appointed by the government, which receives all its profits. It's also true that the Bank of England, set up on his third attempt by the financial adventurer William Paterson in 1694, was also a private company. But it was nationalised in 1946. It is also true that the cock-ups, arrogance and blunders by the world's central banks probably deepened the Great Depression, but that is incompetence not conspiracy. Central banks keep a watchful eye over the world financial system, but can they do anything about it when something goes wrong?

*"I believe that banking institutions are more dangerous to our liberties than standing armies... The issuing power should be taken from the banks and restored to the people to whom it properly belongs."*
Thomas Jefferson

Free market think tanks like the Cato Institute still dream of life without central banks, where market forces can shift money easily from place to place. But there would then be almost no institutions left to provide financial stability in our daily financial roller-coaster rides, with electronic money pouring across the computer screens of the youthful traders of London, Tokyo and New York.

Originally, the central bankers tried to do this by buying up gold as the First World War approached. By the mid 1990s, the United States had managed to buy or borrow half the gold ever mined, and kept it in the vaults of Fort Knox and the Federal Reserve. And there much of it stays, under the streets of New York City, protected by 200 tons of wrought-ironwork around the windows and a private army in the cellars.

The trouble is, this just doesn't work any more. At a whiff of financial trouble around the world, somebody's central bank can totter. Japanese banks have been bailed out three times since the 1980s; the American banks needed the biggest bail-out in history when the 'savings and loans' (building societies) all collapsed in the 1980s. The World Bank cites 69 countries with banking crises since the end of the 1970s, and 87 countries have faced runs on their currency. Sometimes, of course, the markets are right. But they tend to over-correct, with devastating consequences (see pXX)

The former banker, Bernard Lietaer, has calculated that in the mid-1980s, if 5% of the big currency traders sold your currency, it meant a $3 billion pressure that most central banks could withstand. Now, with $2,000 billion changing hands every day, 5% would mean facing an avalanche of $100 billion against your currency – and no central bank can hold out against that. "Today," he says, "all the combined reserves of all the central banks together (about $1,300 billion) ... would be gobbled up in less than a day of normal trading." The prospect is terrifying.

**What can we do about it?**
- Set aside more reserves
- Tax currency speculation with the Tobin Levy (see p 133)
- Set up a global stability currency (see p 144)

*Foreign exchange transactions every day*

| | |
|---|---|
| *1975* | *$15 bn* |
| *1983* | *$60 bn* |
| *1998* | *$1,500 bn* |
| *2000* | *$2,000 bn* |

Bernard Lietaer
*The Future of Money*
Century, 2001
ISBN 0712699910

# Disembodied money

## Trading ether

*"Like trading ether."*
*Rogue trader Nick Leeson's verdict on a world where the New York Mercantile Exchange could trade 200 million barrels of oil – four times the actual amount that exists in the world.*

In the days of the gold standard, of Dreadnoughts and Sherlock Holmes, the balance of world payments was organised every night under the vaults of the world's great banks – with the exhausting work of shifting gold bars from the British cage to the French cage, and so on.

It doesn't happen like that any more. Since Margaret Thatcher ended exchange controls in 1979, and since the 'Big Bang' of deregulation in the City of London, the financial system has become a wild electronic phenomenon managed by a gigantic network of global computers. Money isn't metallic any more: it is bytes and bytes of information about debt, shooting around the world at the rate of $2,000 billion a day.

That's why the British Chancellor Norman Lamont could describe Black Wednesday in 1992 – when the pound was forced out of the European Monetary System – as like "being overwhelmed by a whirlwind".

It's a system that's defended, not by locks and security guards, but by computer codes. Financial decisions often have to be taken in seconds. Computers even buy and sell automatically at different market levels. The real world of goods and services is now dwarfed by the speculative world more than 20 times over.

Trade is no longer the purpose of money. A generation ago, speculation made up a third of what was spent on goods and services. Now trade is dwarfed by a cascade of speculation in stocks, bonds, futures and, most of all, foreign currency – which grows by nearly a quarter every year. The world financial system is in the hands of greedy 24-year-olds in Wall Street and the City of London, who profit hugely from instability.

Worse still, when a successful dealer like the disgraced Michael Milken (see p 127) could earn a reputed $1.5 million a day in the late 1980s dealing in junk bonds, there is less and less incentive for anyone to work in the real economy of goods and services – still less as a teacher or a nurse. In other words, unreality pays.

The consequences for the real world are sometimes terrifying. Black Wednesday wiped 25% off the value of British business in one day, but the next morning everything was just the same – the same buildings, products and staff at their desks. But a catastrophic loss of belief had made them that much less valuable.

When the Asian currency crisis hit Indonesia in 1998, again nothing real had changed and yet soldiers threw hospital patients out onto the street at bayonet point because the hospital's dollar debt was no longer sustainable.

Image is central to the post-modern world of electronic money, and so is belief. If the world believes something is valuable, then it is, just as the audiences for Peter Pan manage to revive Tinkerbell just by believing in her.

That's the modern financial system for you, and we have to live with it. But we have to remember that the power the world of virtual money has over us is given by us. We chose it and can choose otherwise.

Joel Kurtzman
*The Death of Money*
Simon & Schuster, 1993
ISBN 0671687999

# The stock markets

## The world's Big Bangs

*"Speculators may do no harm as bubbles on a steady stream of enterprise. But the position is serious when enterprise becomes the bubble on the whirlpool of speculation. When the capital development of a country becomes a by-product of a casino, the job is likely to be ill-done."*
John Maynard Keynes

The great stock markets of London, New York and Tokyo – and their smaller cousins like the Dax and the Nasdaq – are increasingly the primary focus of the world. Policy-makers, bankers and traders stay glued to the ticker tape with the stock market fluctuations, or the new financial TV channels like Bloomberg, as if their lives depended on it – and in the hope of glimpsing a trend that will, for a few minutes, provide them with an opportunity for profit.

It's a disturbing phenomenon, the world's growing dependence on this giant betting shop. Through our pensions and insurance, we all have a stake in its fluctuations. And, while the collapse of the markets in 1929 led indirectly to the Second World War, we are so much more dependent on those market twitches – and the Just In Time delivery systems for our food – that a comparable collapse today could have devastating, and unpredictable, consequences.

In the Irish potato famine of the 1840s many starved because they only had the potato, and only one blight-infested variety at that. In the 21st century our dependence on money means that if money fails, we, too, have precious few systems to fall back on.

Despite the astonishing attention which stock markets get these days, there is a great deal of mythology about what they do and how.

**It's not really about investment:** The main role of the stock markets is no longer to provide investment capital for business. When shares are sold for the first time, that's what they do – but after that, the rises and falls are just rises and falls. They produce no extra money for the business whose shares are traded, just for the pension funds and investors who are speculating.

**It's not very wise:** Investment decisions are not always made by wise experts, though it may look like that. Much of the buying and selling is done automatically by computer when the markets reach a certain level. And as we saw during the dot.com fiasco (see page 129), many recommendations to buy by the financial advisers in the big merchant banks were influenced by whether or not their bank was involved in the share issue.

**It's not objective:** The markets are not the objective guides to the value of companies they claim to be. During the dot.com explosion, the Dow Jones Index on Wall Street reached a peak of over 11,000 points. It only reached 1,000 points in 1972, and was soon ballooning at a rate of 1,000 points a year, increasing by a third in 1997 alone. Was this an objective measure of the value of American companies? I don't think so.

Powerful stock market valuations do not mean that companies are genuinely valuable. Maybe they are just trendy, like the dot.coms. Maybe they are up to their eyeballs in debt just to scare off corporate raiders who might use their spare borrowing capacity to buy them up (the basis for leveraged buy-outs, see p 127). Maybe they are just being used as collateral to borrow more money to buy more shares because the market will just carry on rising (it will, won't it?).

THE PAST
THE PRESENT
THE FUTURE
ASK RAJAH!

It doesn't mean anything: Nor are the fluctuations a rational basis for looking at the health of the world economy. Nobel prizes in economics are now given to theorists looking for regular, predictable patterns in the share markets. Anything from the movement of the astrological spheres to the behaviour of detergent molecules has been used to work out how the markets behave. Many securities firms and US banks use clairvoyants and astrologers.

It's not a public service: Don't think that traders and clients are somehow on the same side either. "When an account called to say hello, I needed to be prepared to blow his head off and make a sale," said Morgan Stanley trader Frank Partnoy in his book *F.I.A.S.C.O,* describing the sale of a useless Mexican peso-linked derivative issued by an offshore company that collapsed in 1994.

People take the market mythology too seriously. The price of land in Tokyo inflated ten times over during the 1980s, which made its owners into the biggest banks in the world. Japanese companies, too, could use it as collateral to buy up companies all over the globe. The result: overwhelming and unsustainable debt that still threatens to drag down the biggest banks in Japan, and the rest of the world's economy with them.

So companies are not as stable as they look. The top hundred companies in the world control assets of about $3,500 billion, yet since Charles Dow and Edward Jones invented their Dow Jones Index in 1896 only one company has survived (General Electric). All the rest have been dissolved, broken up by the corporate raiders and their once powerful names forgotten.

In the days when we quite rightly accuse corporations of abusing their enormous power, it's worth remembering what is even more powerful than they are: money, banking and financial services.

Conclusion: the financial markets are not so wise after all.

John Gray
*False Dawn: The delusions of global capitalism*
Granta Books, 1998
ISBN 1862075301

# Insurance

## The perils of keeping us safe

It isn't a pleasant experience when your house burns down or someone steals your car. But the thought that we might not lose financially – albeit after a few months battling with our insurance company – is at least a bit of a comfort.

health insurance in some countries you would be on the streets if you became ill. The problems began when insurance companies made assumptions about people in different 'categories'.

Insurance began in ancient Babylon but hardly caught on. In 17th century London it took off; the idea was to insure ship-owners against loss. By 1688, Edward Lloyd was running a coffee house where London merchants and bankers met informally to do business: the result was the foundation of Lloyd's of London and the beginnings of modern insurance.

*"It is not in giving life but in risking life that man is raised above the animal."*
Simone de Beauvoir, *The Second Sex*

By the 20th century, insurance was a necessity. Motor insurance was compulsory, you needed buildings insurance to buy a house, and without

In the USA, anyone from an ethnic minority was assumed to be a bad risk. Anyone with a foreign-sounding name was refused insurance. One 1933 report warned that even accepting a name like 'Ellis' was risky, because some people with that name turned out to be from the Middle East. Underwriting manuals used to include maps with red lines drawn on them to show African-American neighbourhoods where no policies should be sold. As recently as 1962, a Manhattan insurance company was alleged to have used maps on which large areas of various New York boroughs were shaded in with a red crayon.

Red-lining was outlawed in the USA and banks and insurance companies on both sides of the Atlantic vigorously deny it still goes on. And yet a solid 10% of the British population still can't get bank accounts, let alone insurance. President Carter's Community Reinvestment Act of 1977 forced banks to reveal where they lend money, and to pay large sums if they fail to lend it where they accept deposits. The UK government has resisted anything like that.

But insurers are still in the front line:

• The rising number of claims from no-win/no-fee lawyers means that villages and small companies are cancelling events – whether they are office Christmas parties or fireworks displays – because they can't afford the insurance.

• The identification of genes for heart disease, cancer and other chronic diseases has already led to pressure from insurance companies for genetic screening – and the threat of a new underclass of 'uninsurables' - more red-lining...

• Insurance losses from global warming and the rise of natural disasters were £30 billion in the 1960s (in today's prices) – and may reach £200 billion a year by 2050. That might make insurance completely impossible.

### What can we do about it?

A revival of grassroots insurance for some of our needs (remember the friendly societies) would help keep the big companies on their toes.

---

**Sign of the Times**

When people from Sherston in Wiltshire faced an insurance bill of £2,500 in 2002 for their traditional bonfire night, they replaced the fire with a smoke machine and orange paper.

---

Peter L. Bernstein
*Against the Gods:*
*The remarkable story of risk*
John Wiley, 1997
ISBN 0471295639

# Money flows

## What goes around comes around

*"Money is round, and it rolls away."*
Confucius

It isn't just a matter of how much money there is in your country or neighbourhood; it's a question of where it flows to, who gets it, and whether it stays put. What if it pops in but seeps out again to be invested in offshore trusts or arms manufacturing?

That's the insight into money you get when you put aside the idea that it is just about precious metal. If you look at a neighbourhood and count up the money in its collective bank accounts you might get a very distorted idea about who is rich and who is poor. But if you look at whether the money stays put, circulating around – and putting the community to work – you get a much clearer picture.

Money that stays circulating locally is like lifeblood: it keeps communities alive. It brings together the people who need things doing with the people who have time and the raw materials needed. Otherwise things just grind to a halt and die.

This is known as the Multiplier Effect and it was described first by a disciple of Keynes and applied to nations. But conventional economists and governments haven't yet accepted that the same applies to cities and communities too.

Take two communities:

• One has a supermarket, which pays some of its takings to local employees, then banks the rest to be invested in the money markets. Studies of very dependent communities, like native American reservations in the USA, have found that 75 % of their money leaves again within 48 hours – to pay bills to distant utilities, or to shop in Wal-mart, which sends all their takings every night to Arkansas.

• The other community has a range of small shops, and when any of the shopkeepers need something, they can buy it locally. What is earned by one shop is used in the next and so on. Not only is the town centre vibrant and alive, but the small businesses are in charge of their own destiny. Their owners haven't been transformed into reluctant employees by dominant supermarkets.

Both neighbourhoods might have the same amount of money coming in, but one is an economic desert and the other is thriving, sustainable and 'real'. Where a 'supermarket' community is thriving it is only because it has sucked the life out of surrounding communities - whose shops have died.

A study by the New Economics Foundation in Cornwall found that a pound spent on the local vegetable box scheme multiplied in the local economy nearly twice as far as a pound spent in the local supermarket. And when Knowlsey Council in Merseyside measured their local multiplier effect, they found their local economy had become a seriously leaky bucket – only 8% of their expenditure even reached local people.

All the rest was siphoned off by consultants, big corporations and outside contractors.

How do you plug the leaks? You make sure that when investment comes to your community, it behaves like a funnel towards local business. You also take a critical look at investment that might be worth far more, but acts like an umbrella – shooting the money off to outsiders so that it barely reaches local people.

The sad fact is that most modern investment is more like an umbrella than a funnel. The trickle down effect – the idea that money spent on the rich will eventually trickle down to the poor – simply doesn't work. At best the poor receive just that - a trickle.

We invest vast sums in regeneration schemes or attracting foreign factories that so often just benefit the intermediaries involved. At the first sign of an economic downturn, the investments collapse or the factory owners are off to a better deal somewhere else on the globe. A diverse local range of local businesses are more likely to stay put, more likely to spread the wealth around, and more likely to create a sense of local well-being, than a couple of large retailers run by a board of 'fat-cat' directors in London or New York.

This isn't an argument against trade. But it's a reminder that the poorest places often have buying power and assets of their own that the big markets ignore, and which they can use to regenerate themselves.

*Amount spent at a supermarket to create one local job: £250,000*

*Amount spent at a corner shop to create one local job: £50,000*

UK taxpayers' subsidies to build 500 de Lorean cars: £77m

UK taxpayers' subsidies to car-maker, British Leyland: £2,500m

Pay-offs to failed UK directors of FTSE 100 companies since the stock market began falling in 2000: £170m.

Bermie Ward and Julie Lewis
*Plugging the Leaks:
Making the most of every pound that
enter your local economy*
New Economics Foundation, 2002
ISBN 1899407529

# The growth of e-cash

## The rise of the electronic blip

*"We have a problem trying to define exactly what money is... the current definition of money is not sufficient to give us a good means for controlling the money supply."*
Alan Greenspan, chairman of the US Federal Reserve, in testimony to Congress, 17 February 2000

Can money become any more disembodied than it already is? Yes, it can. In fact, we should now hold onto our seats as the money world blasts off from planet earth altogether.

The interest demanded from investments is already way beyond anything that the natural world can produce – so must be unsustainable. The products traded by Wall Street and the City of London often don't exist in the real world. Traders might buy copper futures – the right to buy copper at a set price on a set future date – which bear no relation to the actual amount of copper in the world. Derivatives are even more surreal (see p 131).

Only 3% of money in circulation is 'real' notes and cash; the rest is just debits on a computer. But even cash is beginning to be replaced by bytes on smartcards. In Finland you can buy a Coke from a drinks dispenser or pay a parking meter by phoning it up – and the price gets debited on your mobile phone bill.

McDonalds, Microsoft and a range of other corporates have even experimented with their own electronic money. Internet currencies like beenz.com and i-points briefly thrived online. There are now seven trillion unused frequent flyer points and Air Miles in the world.

E-cash isn't necessarily a bad thing; it means we don't have to fiddle around with heavy, expensive coins. Paying for small items electronically is more convenient and cheaper. It costs over £250 million a year to mint, transport and guard the cash in the UK.

When they shifted over to the euro, it took 80 lorries a day for three months to haul out the old coins – and that was just in Belgium.

But we have to be careful with e-cash. If there is less of the hard stuff in circulation, then there's less for the poorest people who rely on it most. We won't be able to give money to beggars, perhaps, unless they have their own card reader for an electronic transfer. And in a world where corporations know precisely where their customers come from, we may get branded money that, because of the rules attached to it, will circulate easily from mobile phone to the internet and smartcard, but simply avoid poor people altogether.

The future of e-cash is that it's likely to be issued by transport companies, retailers, phone companies and utilities, because they have the infrastructure to handle enormous transactions. They will probably join forces to issue different competing brands, maybe competing to put them onto local government smartcards like the new one being issued for London Underground passengers. It's a complicated business, of codes and keys and validation, running your own electronic money – a little like voting. Indeed the patent for one of the first digital currencies, DigiCash, has been adapted to run voting systems.

But it's important that not all money be electronic or branded. The key to a fairer money system is having lots of different kinds of money (see p 164). The fewer kinds of money there are, the more they can get hi-jacked by the wealthy.

*Paul Gosling*
*Changing Money:*
*How the digital age is*
*transforming financial services*
Bowerdean Publishing, 1999
ISBN 0906097452

# Offshore banking

## Where did all the money go?

*"There is simply no available skilled labour, and the cost structures are prohibitive for most other industries. The banking cuckoo has taken over the nest."*
John Christensen, former economic advisor to Jersey

It's a mystery worthy of Agatha Christie, and it is made possible by the way that money has transformed itself into information. Where, for example, are the missing chunks of the 1998 $4.8 billion IMF loan to Russia, most of which disappeared soon after its arrival?

The answer is that most of it left the Russian economy via the secretive and anonymous circuits of the offshore finance centres, to re-enter the capital markets in private hands, invested respectably in London and New York.

Most of these offshore centres are tiny pin-pricks on an atlas, like Jersey, the Bahamas, the British Virgin Islands or Labuan in Malaysia – though Luxembourg, Switzerland and even offshore aspects of London, New York and Dublin should be included as well. These tiny places now host a staggering amount of the world's wealth.

Because of the secrecy that surrounds them – the Jersey authorities prefer the term 'confidentiality' – we can't know how much. A recent estimate is around $6-8,000 billion, nearly the equivalent of the entire annual world trade in goods and services, or about one third of all global wealth. Deposits held in the Channel Isles and the Isle of Man probably now amount to an astonishing £400 billion. Again, it's secret – but at one stage the Conservative Party maintained 40 offshore accounts around the world.

Meanwhile, vast sums of speculative capital flows through the offshore centres, unregulated and beyond the control of nation states. In Jersey and Guernsey, non-resident companies can negotiate tax rates of less than 2%, which is why multinationals like Rupert Murdoch's News International are able to avoid almost all tax. Tax avoidance in the USA now runs at about $325 billion a year, mostly via offshore tax shelters.

Then there are the drug lords, black marketeers and mafiosi using the offshore centres to launder their ill-gotten gains. Cyprus alone handles about $2.5 billion a year from the Russian black economy. Organised crime is now worth about $1,500 billion a year around the world.

But, even for the small islands, it's risky. Jersey's economic advisor John Christensen warned that the island's offshore banking was pricing out all other economic activities. Tourism is suffering, and there is almost no agriculture left. The cost of living and owning property has been hiked by the offshore banks.

This 'cuckoo in the nest effect' affects anyone living next to a big financial centre – like London. In the end, financial services start driving everything else out. The capture of Jersey by the awesome power of world capital is a warning to Britain, where economic policy is tailored to the financial services industry, while manufacturing struggles away unsupported. Perhaps the fate of Jersey is a frightening vision of the future for us all.

*Money known to be in the world's private banks:*

|  |  |
|------|--------|
| *1986* | *$4,300 bn* |
| *1997* | *$10,000 bn* |
| *2000* | *$13,000 bn* |

*Source: Gemini Consulting*

*Kavalijt Singh*
*Taming Global Capital Flows:*
*Challenges and alternatives in the era of*
*financial globalisation: a citizen's guide*
Zed Books, 2000
ISBN 1856497844

# Ownership

## The hidden power of money

*"The economy of the future is based on relationships rather than possession."*
John Perry Barlow

It can work both ways. Turning money into information can make it more available: it can help us find out what we need to support ourselves and it can change the whole nature of the money system. It isn't solid like metal: when you sell information, you still keep it yourself – it's just worth a bit less than it was before.

But it can also work the other way around. When money becomes information, then ownership rights get extended from things like land and property to ideas, information, music and words. Both processes have accelerated over the past generation and the growth of 'intellectual property' has echoed with the giant sucking sound of multinationals hoovering up income from the use of their 'intellectual property' all over the world.

Patents are sometimes important: they allow companies to invest heavily in new medicines, without worrying about people stealing them once they have got them through the regulators. But the greedy exploitation of rights can undermine innovation in other places. The whole basis of the wealth of some medieval cities was copying and improving the goods they imported, with dramatic consequences: funnelling the wealth of the world to the already rich.

It is bad enough when patent rules make it impossible, for example, for Third World countries to develop their own generic Aids drugs. But the World Trade Organisation's TRIPS agreement takes this process to whole new levels. TRIPS rules can threaten the livelihoods of poor farmers by handing over control to corporations of local plant genetic resources. By patenting certain traits in genes, seeds and plants, companies can acquire monopoly rights to produce and market important seeds and the inputs needed to grow them. The increases in prices for seeds that result can destroy the livelihoods of poor farmers.

The trouble is that TRIPS is based on Northern understandings of knowledge and ownership. It does not protect indigenous people and farmers, whose intellectual property tends to belong to the whole community and is often part of their culture and spirituality. More than half of the world's most frequently-prescribed drugs are derived from plants or synthetic copies of plant chemicals. One estimate says that if indigenous farmers around the world were paid just 2% royalties on genetic resources they have developed, big pharmaceutical companies would owe more than $5 billion in unpaid royalties for medicinal plants alone.

The most notorious example was the Neem Tree. In 1994 the American company W.R. Grace won the patent for a fungicide derived from the seeds of the Neem tree, which is traditionally used in Asia, Africa, Central and South America as an insect repellent for crops. The patent was revoked by the European Patent Office in May 2000 on the grounds that it was not a new technology – but, elsewhere, the injustice continues.

Like basmati rice. A company called RiceTec from Texas managed to patent basmati rice grown anywhere in the Western hemisphere – and any blending of Pakistani or Indian basmati strains with other kinds of rice that had been created by farmers there. Basmati rice strains had been developed for generations by Punjabi farm families. In fact the strains had been donated originally to the Washington-based International Food Policy Research Institute. A massive campaign by representatives of indigenous farmers persuaded the US patent office to throw out RiceTec's remaining claims.

Worse, the demand for profitable patents means that big pharmaceutical companies tend to invest in research for profitable drugs – small improvements for Northern complaints like impotence rather than major leaps forward for Southern problems like malaria. Aids drugs have mainly been targeted at Northern strains of the disease, rather than the strains that are devastating Africa. Other abuses include:

• More than 40 pharmaceutical companies sued the South African government for importing cheap copies (known as generics) of Aids medicines. They later withdrew.

• Pharmaceutical giant Glaxo SmithKline also bullied and threatened Ghana and Uganda for importing generic drugs for Aids.

• The USA took Brazil to the WTO disputes procedure, for flouting TRIPS by producing a generic copy of AZT drugs, which cost a mere $3,000 a year, instead of the $15,000 charged in the US. The cheaper drug allowed 60,000 Aids sufferers in Brazil to receive free treatment.

The problem is wider than patents. By investing in foreign companies, corporations take a lifetime's rights over them. They are slowly extending permanent ownership over increasingly wide swathes of the world. What can be done to hand back ownership to people, now that we know nationalisation doesn't really work?

Here are three ideas:

• **Rights that expire:** According to the Australian financier Shann Turnbull, permanent rights are inefficient – no company looks beyond 20 years, so the system is over-paying them. The alternative, he suggests, is for rights to investments to expire after 20 years and revert to a local trust that would pay a dividend to every citizen every year (see p 106).

• **Citizen's royalties:** every citizen of Alaska gets an annual dividend from the Alaskan Permanent Fund, of about $2,000 a year, paid out from the oil revenues.

• **Free shares:** the respected financial journalist Samuel Brittan has suggested handing out free shares from privatisations to people, as of right – since they did theoretically own the big utilities in the first place.

*The Free Lunch*
Charles Bazlinton
Orchard Four, 2002
ISBN 0954410505

# Globalisation

## Rule by money

*"The current status quo only measures money. It's a kind of survival of the economically fittest. But their interpretation of the 'fit' – the marketable, the profitable, the global – is pathetically inadequate. The financially 'fit' survive. Those that don't fit - people, communities and nations - are bled dry. It's a devastating machine that can bear no variation, and it isn't building the kind of world most of us want."*
Anita Roddick, 2001

The corporate pioneer John D. Rockefeller once boasted that he was quite willing to pay someone a salary of a million dollars if he were brutal enough. "He must be able to glide over every moral restraint with almost

childlike disregard," he wrote, "and have, besides other positive qualities, no scruples whatsoever and be ready to kill thousands of victims – without a murmur." That is one aspect of the phenomenon known as 'globalisation': the rather adolescent belief that, somehow, morality doesn't apply to the world of business and finance – that, alone among the human race, the financial masters of the universe have only one duty, to their shareholders.

A second aspect is the perversion of the idea of free trade – an idea originally invented by Victorian Liberals as the next stage in the campaign against slavery, so that free people could trade with each other equally, as a vital defence against monopoly. Now the same idea is used to justify the precise opposite – the right of the most powerful in the world to dominate the powerless, and as a way to make the world safe for monopolist corporations.

But a third aspect is what makes globalisation so powerful, and why it belongs in this section. It is powered by the rapid movement of capital electronically from one side of the world, almost instantly – a devastating punishment for countries that step out of line. Their currencies can collapse.

The result is a system, subsidised and abetted by governments, that hands power to a handful of transnational corporations, turning the world into a playground for those who can move capital and projects quickly from place to place. It is the dubious idea that business can make everyone better off by roaming from country to country with no restrictions – in search of the lowest wages, the loosest environmental regulations, the most docile and desperate workers. This is a world of nomadic capital that never sets down roots, never builds communities, and leaves little behind but toxic waste and embittered workers.

Globalisation is many things, not all of them disastrous. The ability to see into previously hidden hell-holes all over the world is a force for moral good. Dictators are exposed. But the rule of one culture over another, driven by the ferocious kind of globalisation that insists that the people of the world trade because they have to, not because they want to, is another matter altogether.

Enforcing this vision is the unaccountable World Trade Organisation (WTO) on the shores of Lake Geneva, deciding on food safety or environmental impact in closed and secret sessions. Many small countries can't afford to keep delegations there and are thus excluded. The results are everywhere to see, in the inability of small governments to spend on education or health, or to regulate flows of capital in and out – often imposed as 'structural adjustment' as part of debt rescheduling – and the sinking of whole populations, rich and poor alike, into pathetic dependence. For example:

• Tribal people can no longer draw water from the ancient tank at Maharashtra in India, because it has been sold exclusively to Coca-Cola. The World Bank has been pressurising India to privatise even more water.

• Pepsi has been trying to prevent local people storing

water on their roofs elsewhere in India. Collecting rainwater has been made illegal in parts of Bolivia after it was forced to sell its water industry to a subsidiary of the US giant Bechtel.

• The WTO has ruled that nations may not discriminate between tuna caught without killing dolphins and tuna caught by those who don't care, or to discriminate against beef given growth hormones, even though they have a built-in price advantage over healthy, natural beef.

• Seed monopolists Monsanto have prosecuted small farmers for hoarding seeds to plant the following year – the traditional method. They have also been developing seeds that will only grow in conjunction with their own patent pesticides.

• A group of Nicaragua workers have been indicted on charges carrying 10 years in jail because they asked for a $0.08 increase per pair of jeans they assemble for retailers like Wal-mart, selling at $30 each in the USA.

The symptoms of aggressive globalisation are all around us, but nowhere more so than in the enforced dependence of the poorest people of the world. "The imperative to stamp out the smallest insect, the smallest plant, the smallest peasant comes from a deep fear," writes the Indian physicist Vandana Shiva, "the fear of everything that is alive and free."

The WTO has some potential to support the poorest. But not until they are reformed so that poor countries can afford to use their mechanisms properly. And not until it shares responsibility for enforcing environmental agreements.

*Countries vs corporations (GDP or total sales):*

| | |
|---|---|
| General Motors | $162 bn |
| Thailand | $152 bn |
| Norway | $150 bn |
| Ford | $145 bn |
| Mitsui | $142 bn |
| Saudi Arabia | $138 bn |
| South Africa | $128 bn |
| Shell | $126 bn |
| Wal-mart | $117 bn |
| Malaysia | $98 bn |
| Israel | $98 bn |

Anita Roddick
*Take it Personally:
How globalisation affects you
and how to fight back*
Thorsons, 2001
ISBN 0007128983

Section III

# Measuring money

The trouble with money is that it isn't a very good measuring rod. It gives a high value to useless things (Dunkin' Donuts), to dangerous things (stealth bombers) and to fleeting things (Versace trinkets), but places very little value on the really important things like loving, caring human beings. Yet we give it central importance in the management of the world.

# The first accountants

## Pacioli and book-keeping

*"Use figures as little as you can. Remember your client doesn't like or want them, he wants brains. Think and act upon facts, truths and principles and regard figures only as things to express these, and so proceeding you are likely to become a great accountant and a credit to one of the truest and finest professions in the land."*
James Anyon, the first accountant in the USA

The first accountants were the philosopher-priests of ancient times, who kept tallies and worked the abacus, mysteriously and with peculiar ritual hand movements, coming up with an answer that nobody could challenge.

What transformed this basic measuring system was the Italian renaissance, and the need for the new merchants to keep track of their international deals while they were making the two-year voyages to India and back, and to see whether they were profitable or not.

They did so using three new inventions:
**Paper**, which allowed people to do calculations that were written down for all to see, rather that the mysterious hocus-pocus of the abacus users.

**Zero**, a whole new concept borrowed from the Arabs along with their numerals, banned by the Church in 1229 because of its satanic sense of nothingness and its fraudulent potential to multiply figures with a slip of the pen. It was then used as an underground symbol of free trade.

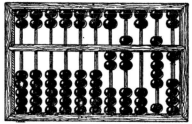

**Double-entry book-keeping**, first explained by a friend of Leonardo da Vinci, the mathematician and Venetian friar Luca Pacioli – who was such good friends with the Pope that he had been given permission to ignore his vow of poverty and own property.

Just as Columbus was sighting the new world, Pacioli sat down and began the book that made him famous, *Summa de arithmetica, geometria, proportioni et proportionalita* (1494) – cramming everything in there from astrology and military tactics to music ("nothing else but proportion and proportionality"). Its section on book-keeping stayed in print for 500 years, still being translated into German and Russian well into the 19th century.

Pacioli developed a way of reducing everything to numbers, but he didn't want accountancy to forget morality and spirituality. He suggested starting each page of the ledger with the cross and with the name of God. Merchants had used a similar system for about two centuries, at least one of them starting each page with the words "For God and for profit".

Later generations forgot that basic respect for things which can't be reduced to money, yet accountants still managed to hang onto the aura of priesthood. As a result, failures of accountancy from the Royal Mail Scandal of the 1920s right through to BCCI, the Maxwell affair and the Enron collapse, have all been greeted with calls for even more accountancy than before.

The trouble is that all rule-based systems of measurement tend to miss the point. That's one reason why the tick-box style of American accountancy, known as Generally Agreed Accountancy Principles (or GAAP), failed so spectacularly to pick up the fact that, while Enron may have been the most innovative company in the USA, it was also cooking the books.

Alfred Crosby
*The Measure of Reality:
Quantification and Western
society 1250-1600*
Cambridge University Press, 1997
ISBN 0521639905

# The last accountants

## The curse of Enron

We tend to see accountants as quiet, retiring and objective professionals, and of course they often are. But almost unnoticed behind them stand four global organisations with immense power: the mega-accountancy firms, Deloitte Touche Tohmatsu, Ernst & Young, KPMG and PricewaterhouseCoopers, and they are not retiring at all.

Between them they audit all the FTSE 100 companies and employ over half a million people, with revenues – before the Enron affair, when there were five of them – of over $65 billion every year. They are not just auditors, but providers of management services, and purveyors of the latest management fads, from downsizing to re-engineering. They are also the cheer-leaders for globalisation.

> *"The sense of responsibility in the financial community for the community is not small. It is nearly nil."*
> John Kenneth Galbraith, *The Great Crash* 1929

Enron collapsed in 2002, followed shortly afterwards by their auditors Arthur Andersen, which had been paid $25 million the previous year for services over and above their basic accounting, and which ended the relationship to the sound of the shredding of documents. The Big Four had just lived through an insane period of corporate history – partly their own responsibility – that led to American accountants increasingly employing tick-box methods of checking accounts that allowed so much wrong-doing to slip past public scrutiny.

In the days when more than 90% of the value of a company like Microsoft could be made up of intangibles – brand value, know-how, belief in future profits – then the world needed innovative accountancy.

Unfortunately, it got the wrong kind of innovation. The Big Four have:

**Facilitated the concentration of corporate power.** When a KPMG report found that 83% of corporate mergers produced no benefits, and half actually made the companies involved poorer – though not of course the deal-makers in the Big Four – managers tried, and failed, to suppress it.

**Built up cosy relationships with their audit clients** – and that got in the way of proper public scrutiny.

**Aided aggressive tax minimisation** for the biggest companies in the world, via legal tax havens and other tricks. They have thus been undermining the ability of democratic governments to get things done. The UK government alone estimates it loses up to $25 billion a year in this kind of tax avoidance.

**Earned about £22 million from the UK aid budget** (1999-2000) for consultancy and advice (that figure applied when they were the Big Five, including Arthur Andersen).

**Contributed $13 million to political funds** in the US election year of 2000, including $700,000 to George W. Bush.

*Number of accountants in the UK*

| | |
|---|---|
| *1904* | *6,000* |
| *1957* | *38,000* |
| *1999* | *109,000* |

Andrew Simms
*Five Brothers:*
*The rise and nemesis of the big bean counters*
New Economics Foundation, 2002
ISBN 1889407456

# The lunacy of GDP

## Why money isn't everything

*"We destroy the beauty of the countryside because the unappropriated splendours of nature have no economic value. We are capable of shutting off the sun and the stars because they do not pay a dividend."*
John Maynard Keynes, *National Self-Sufficiency, 1933*

It was the 1955 British general election that introduced the concept of 'economic growth' to UK politics. It was an innovation of the Chancellor of the Exchequer, R. A. Butler, and was based on the work of wartime economists like Keynes and Simon Kuznets, who developed 'national accounts' as a way to beat Hitler.

The idea was simple. If you can grow the value of goods and services going through the economy by 3% a year – a pernicious total known as Gross National Product (GNP) or Gross Domestic Product (GDP) – then you could double people's standard of living in a quarter of a century.

The trouble was that it wasn't true. GDP wasn't a measure of the standard of living at all (see p 68), it was a measure of the value of stuff going through the economy – a very different thing. Maybe all the money was being used cleaning up pollution or oil spillages, or solving murders, or chopping down trees to make into paper cartons for fast food. GDP would then be higher, but life certainly wouldn't be 'richer' – it would just mean there were more spillages and more murder.

This terrible mistake was built into government policy all over the world. If GDP went up, governments could take more money in tax and pay for more. Soon the only figure that mattered to officials was GDP, and for economists it was just about measuring economic activity, but politicians used it as a sort of Holy Grail.

There are other problems with GDP as an instrument of policy:

**It doesn't measure everything**: all is well as long as money is changing hands. If money isn't changing hands, it doesn't get measured. Looking after old people at home isn't counted; paying for their nursing homes is.

**It takes no account of natural wealth**: when a tree is growing it isn't included in GDP; only when it's chopped up for toothpicks does it get into the national accounts.

**It encourages fatuous ideas about progress**: Anyone who questions GDP – whether it is better to protect wetlands or forests than to replace them with an airport – is told that GDP is 'progress' and you shouldn't stand in its way.

**It makes no sense of spirituality**: GDP is used to assess developing countries: but how can you measure the success of a country when their most important product is prayer and monks?

**It tries to work both ways**: GDP goes up when people over-eat fast food, then goes up again when they have operations to make them look thin again. It goes up with sales of pesticides that cause cancer and again with sales of drugs to cure it – perhaps by the same company. People in Los Angeles spend a total of $800 million a year just on the petrol they use up in traffic jams. Is that 'progress'?

**It doesn't measure unpaid work**, and most of it is done by women and in the home. When you marry your housekeeper, said the New Zealand MP Marilyn Waring, GDP goes down.

At the foot of the list of male economists who helped develop the concept of GDP in the 1930s under Kuznets, was found this note: "Five clerks, all women with substantial experience and know-how, assisted importantly in this work." These anonymous women – all with substantial experience apparently – had become non-persons and their invisibility had spread to the system they created which still ignores women's work.

But GDP is more destructive than that. Because if that is all governments measure, then they actually become blind to anything else, whether it is the environment or quality of life. And sure enough, if you don't measure the good things in life, then some get concreted over and soon don't exist anyway.

Even Simon Kuznets began to have second thoughts. "The welfare of a nation can scarcely be inferred from a measurement of national income as defined above," he warned in 1934. Nearly 30 years later, he went much further: "Distinctions must be kept in mind between quantity and quality of growth, between its costs and return, and between the short and the long run. Goals for 'more' growth should specify more growth of what and for what."

There's nothing wrong with GDP as a measurement. But it gets to be a problem when it is all we measure. It matters that GDP fell during the 1990s in 54 countries, but the solution won't just be 'more growth'.

---

*UK people active in the voluntary sector (not in GDP):* **23 million**

*UK people in paid work:* **22 million**

---

The GDP of Ladakh (Eastern Kashmir) is among the lowest in the world, nearly nil per person. Yet Ladakh is considered by many to be one of the world's most balanced, sustainable and happy societies. Assessed by GDP, it is a basket-case.
*Helena Nerburg-Hodge: "Ancient Futures"*

---

Marilyn Waring
*If Women Counted: A new feminist economics*
HarperCollins, 1989
ISBN 0062509403

# Happiness

## Why money isn't a very good guide

*"Money can't buy you love."*
Lennon and McCartney

With all the emphasis politicians and economists put on GDP and growth – and the crucial importance of "not standing in the way of progress" – you might think there was some kind of link with human fulfilment and happiness.

There is little to link rising income in itself with rising happiness, and a lot of evidence that despite accelerating incomes, the degree of happiness has stayed much the same in Western nations for the past half century or so. If rich people are happier (it can happen), it usually is to do with their relationships with other people – and perhaps the fact that they have more than us, which is always a source of satisfaction.

In fact, one economist who has studied happiness, Professor Richard Layard, has suggested a wealth tax on very rich people because their wealth causes measurable unhappiness in other people. There is some evidence that 'status' goods, luxury items and designer logos do cause unhappiness in people who can't afford them. They certainly cause envy.

But that is all about relative wealth: there is no direct connection between money and happiness in itself – just between wealth differences and unhappiness.

So why don't policy-makers abandon growth altogether and measure their success in the way that Jeremy Bentham urged them to do – by the greatest happiness of the greatest number? Well, because it is impossible to balance the happiness of the many against the happiness of individuals (you end up, as now, with the happiness of some outweighing the rest). But maybe they should follow people's moods a little more than they follow money, which they do obsessively. If they did that, they might, for example:

**Help people off the 'hedonic treadmill'**: that's the name economists give the exhausting way people work harder, juggle more, stress themselves half to death, in pursuit of material goods that won't make them any happier.

**Put meaning above productivity**: all the evidence is that we need balance in our lives – family, nature, creativity – and that the shift from total stress to total pointlessness in retirement or unemployment is a major source of ill-health.

**Concentrate on mental hygiene**: Mental illness causes half of Britain's disability, but gets only 12% of health resources. Depression is curable but only about a quarter of those suffering from it get treatment.

**Concentrate on public good**: despite rationing and lower incomes during the Second World War, people in Britain were largely happier – because of their efforts for the public good. Despite this, politicians have done much to undermine the remaining ethos of public service. The truth is, it makes people happier.

*The top ten happiest countries in the world (Source: The Economist):*

| | |
|---|---|
| Columbia | Guinea |
| Switzerland | Canada |
| Denmark | Nicaragua |
| Costa Rica | Sweden |
| Iceland | Ireland |

Richard Layard's lectures
http//: cep.lse.ac.uk

# Efficiency

## The cult of incompetence

Why do the railways still break down or doctors and nurses make so many mistakes in hospitals? Why is it so difficult to talk to a human being at a 'customer service' centre long enough – especially if your problem doesn't match any of the available categories on their software? The answer is because, economically, these streamlined modern institutions are 'efficient'.

This doesn't mean efficient in the 'old' sense, that they have the resources to make sure people's needs are met, or that they have enough staff capacity in case people are ill. Nor is it efficiency in the sustainable sense, achieving things with a minimum of resources. What is heralded as efficient these days is often nothing of the kind, because 'efficiency' really means 'value for money'. The train operators employ just enough staff to provide a service as long as nothing goes wrong. The vast hospitals, with hundreds of different disciplines under one roof, simply ignore the side-effects of that kind of inhuman efficiency: patients never seeing the same doctor twice, mistakes because staff don't feel involved, untreatable hospital bugs.

*"For four wicked centuries the world has dreamed this foolish dream of efficiency, and the end is not yet."*
George Bernard Shaw,
*John Bull's Other Island*

Of course, it is right that public services should cost as little as possible, but there came a point – some years ago – when narrow money efficiency, giantism and technocracy were undermining their ability to do the job. Vast hospitals and factory schools are managed from Whitehall by target and indicator, often run at arms-length according to confidential contracts with private companies. The result is a long way from human-scale, and it certainly isn't efficient in its broadest sense.

The cult of efficiency has been spread over the past generation by the big management consultancies, like McKinsey's, or the big accountancy firms (see p 63). Their young consultants, fresh out of business school, are farmed out to help organisations become more 'efficient', and to catch up with whatever the latest management fad happens to be. And at some expense: McKinsey's standard fees are £150,000 to £250,000 a month.

Management consultants now advise the Prime Minister and government departments, just as they so helpfully did to Enron, Global Crossing and other collapsed companies of the post-dot.com era. Their mantra is that everything can be measured, and what can be measured can be managed – which is nonsense.

Notable disasters of the cult of efficiency include:

**Railtrack**: management consultants advised the new owners of Britain's rail infrastructure, Railtrack – privatised for £5 billion – that they should 'sweat their assets' (be more 'efficient' in how often they checked the track). The result was a series of accidents and Railtrack's spectacular collapse.

**Swissair**: McKinsey's advised Swissair to invest $2 billion in small European airlines. Swissair went bankrupt in 2001.

**Hospitals**: mistakes in hospitals rose by a quarter in 2002 alone. One London teaching hospital made 135 mistakes over drugs to patients every week in 2002, a quarter of them serious.

**Call centres**: most UK call centres have now reduced the average length of call to less than a minute – then they wonder why relationships with customers are so bad.

Ironically, these 'externalities' (see p 77) make these vast new bureaucracies more expensive to run, but the real bill falls on someone else.

David Boyle
*The Tyranny of Numbers*
HarperCollins/Flamingo, 2001
ISBN 0006531997

# Measuring what's important 1

## Alternative indicators

*"If your local police chief announced that 'activity' on the streets had increased by 15%, people would not be interested. Exactly what increased? Tree planting or burglaries? Volunteerism or muggings? Car wrecks or neighborly acts of kindness."*
*Atlantic Monthly*, October 1995

There must be better ways of measuring progress than just money, and there are. The King of Bhutan even uses a measure he calls 'gross national contentment'.

Then a group of researchers from the think-tank Redefining Progress put forward an alternative in the American magazine *Atlantic Monthly*. Their article piled on the evidence against GDP. The *Wall Street Journal* had just worked out that O. J. Simpson's trial had cost the equivalent of the

total GDP of Granada. Was that progress? Then there were the liposuction operations – 110,000 of which take place every year in the USA, each of them pumping $2,000 into the growth figures.

The solution was known as the Index of Sustainable Economic Welfare (ISEW). They plotted GDP against it on the same chart. The ISEW showed that, while GDP went up inexorably, sustainable welfare changed direction in the 1970s and started going down. The ISEW for the UK showed a similar decline.

In other words, if you ignore the bottom line of money, we are actually worse off. We are suffering from the opposite of wealth, what John Ruskin called 'illth'.

The ISEW launched a worldwide movement to measure progress more meaningfully. Cities began to use different yardsticks. Seattle used the number of salmon in local streams, the number of books taken out of local libraries and the ratio between McDonalds and vegetarian restaurants. Such indicators became central to Seattle's planning for the future.

In the UK, there was a similar story. Local authorities tried measuring the number of breeding golden eagles (Strathclyde), the asthma rate (Leeds), the amount sold in small shops (West Devon), the number of swans (Norwich). None of them were enough by themselves, but these alternative indicators have been an important counterweight to the narrowness of money. No one measure can sum up all the facets of 'wealth', but these indicators can at least broaden the debate.

This local measuring dovetails well with the very influential UN Human Development Index. Even the UK now has its own battery of sustainability targets.

What next? Finance ministers should be made to report on such things to their parliaments once a year. The UK government now has over 100 indicators of success, but some of them are of dubious value: measuring building on brownfield sites may actually mean scrubbing up the few remaining wildlife areas in cities. Also they have little status within government, and you won't find the Chancellor of the Exchequer announcing them. But change may come.

**One thing that GDP doesn't measure:**
*The USA has lost half its topsoil over the past century.*

Alex Macgillivray, Candy Weston and Catherine Unsworth
*Communities Count! A step-by-step guide to community sustainability indicators*
New Economics Foundation, 1998
ISBN 1899407200

# Measuring what's important 2

## Social auditing

*"Business must be run at a profit, else it will die. But when anyone tries to run a business solely for profit ... then also the business must die, for it no longer has a reason for existence."*
Henry Ford

The 1621 charter of the Dutch West India Company made it responsible for conservation, police and justice. In those days, if you had economic power, you were expected to have moral responsibilities. Over the past century or so, big business philosophy has forgotten that crucial truth, and we can see the results all around us in the devastated environment, poisoned children and degraded lives.

Some solution to this blindness is all the more urgent now that the world's largest corporations account for as much as 28% of global activity – yet only pay 0.25% of the world's population as employees. As their monopoly on economic activity gets sharper, it gets harder for anyone else to sustain themselves outside their corrosive embrace.

Social auditing emerged over the past quarter of a century as a different way of measuring the success of companies. It demands that they look beyond their shareholders to measure their impact on a range of other 'stakeholders' – anyone from employees and their families to regulators, suppliers, neighbours, customers and the environment.

It was the idea of John Elkington, co-author of the 1988 bestseller *The Green Consumer Guide* (see p 174), that every company should have what he called a 'triple bottom line' for their economic, environmental and social achievement. It was all a long way from the days when one of the American 'robber baron' capitalists, Cornelius Vanderbilt, used to keep all his company's figures in his head because he didn't trust anybody.

In the atmosphere of corporate suspicion of the 1990s, social auditing became unexpectedly popular. One new social auditing consultancy reported 50 inquiries a day. Soon the social audits or the unaudited social reports, like the Shell Values report, were pouring off the presses, full of glossy pictures and lofty claims: "We had looked in the mirror and we neither recognised nor liked what we saw," said the Shell Values report. "We have set about putting it right."

Do we believe them? Not quite yet. Social auditing still has some way to go before it becomes mainstream:

**Too much greenwash:** Some social reports are glossy PR efforts that hide the basic unsustainability of everything else the company is doing.

**Too many numbers:** Social auditing has tended to shift responsibility for ethics away from chief executives and over to number-crunchers in the audit department – and, after all, you can't actually measure what's really important.

**Too vague:** Different social reports use different measures. They need to be simpler and more standard before they attract widespread interest.

**Too irrelevant:** Corporate social responsibility remains stuck, because the basic controls on a company are still share price and the money markets – and any company that tries to be more ethical than others, like Levi-Strauss or the Body Shop, can be seriously punished by the money men and the traders.

### What can be done

Globalisation has, at least, introduced 'transparency' into the affairs of corporations. There is pressure now for more stringent reporting, for which legislation has been proposed (the CORE bill).

John Elkington
*Cannibals with Forks: The triple bottom line of 21st century business*
Capstone, 1999
ISBN 1841120847

# Other kinds of capital

## Why it isn't just about money

*"How much would it cost you in real cash terms if none of your employees had ever been toilet-trained?"*
Alvin Toffler, questioning senior US corporate executives

Even the money system grinds to a halt if some of its support structures start to look threadbare.

Old-fashioned economics used to imagine three kinds of capital – land, labour and 'manufactured capital', by which they meant factories, machines, tools and homes. But green economists like Paul Ekins have replaced that with a model of four pillars that underpin real wealth:

**Manufactured capital**: the importance of the buildings we live in, and the infrastructure. We can't make the economy work if the trains keep breaking down.

**Environmental capital**: however much money we might have, we will be grindingly poor if we can't breathe the air and we are the only species on the planet left alive.

**Knowledge capital**: the vital importance of ideas and know-how. If companies don't treat their staff well, their knowledge may just walk out of the door and work for their competitors.

**Social capital**: it is becoming ever clearer just how much everything we try to do depends on a sense of community that works. Doctors can't make people well without the co-operation of their patients and a wider community, the police can't tackle crime, and business profits evaporate if the community malfunctions. One study of social capital found that the number of times tenants visited their GP depended on whether the council scheme to demolish their homes was on or off. And in a massive study in Chicago in 1997, researchers found that crime rates in each neighbourhood had nothing to do with income or unemployment: it was about whether people felt safe enough to intervene when they saw children and teenagers hanging around.

And there in a nutshell is the problem of modern money: it ignores people and the environment. Their destruction as a by-product of economic activity is known blandly as 'externalities'. Small diverse shops nurture social capital, for example; big supermarkets drive it out.

"One ordinary morning last winter," wrote the urban planner Jane Jacobs about her home in New York City 40 years ago, "Bernie Jaffe and his wife Ann supervised the small children crossing at the corner [on the way to school]; lent an umbrella to one customer and a dollar to another; took in some packages for people who were away; lectured two youngsters who asked for cigarettes; gave street directions; took custody of a watch to give the repair man across the street; gave out information on the range of rents in the neighbourhood to an apartment seeker; listened to a tale of domestic difficulty and offered reassurance; told some rowdies they could not come in unless they behaved and then defined (and got) good behaviour; provided an incidental forum for half a dozen conversations among customers who dropped in for oddments; set aside certain newly arrived papers and magazines for regular customers; advised a mother who came for a birthday present not to get the ship-model kit because another child going to the same birthday party was giving that; and got a back copy (this was for me) of the previous day's newspaper out of the deliverer's surplus returns when he came by."

That's social capital. Any institutions that create trust underpin us, and money doesn't work without it.

Paul Ekins, Mayer Hillman and Robert Hutchison
*Wealth Beyond Measure:*
*An atlas of new economics*
Gaia Books, 1992
ISBN 1856750507

# Green taxes

## Taxing the bad things

What can we do about this damage to the fabric of the world, these so-called externalities, that seem to be produced by most economic activity? Some you can make illegal, but some of them you simply can't. Some of them you can tax and, maybe at the same time, shift taxes off the good things like jobs or added value. That means that the polluter would pay for the damage.

Even the laggardly British government has successfully taxed petrol, use of landfill, and now congestion in London. But to do that effectively you have to know what the damage is worth - not precisely but, for political reasons, you need some facts at your finger tips.

*'It was as true as taxes is,' said Mr Barkis, 'And nothing's truer than them.'"*
Charles Dickens, *David Copperfield*

Taxes on cars and petrol in the UK raise around £26 billion, but - contrary to popular opinion - this doesn't cover the real damage that road traffic causes. According to the environmental economist David Pearce, once you have factored in policing, health effects, the cost of injuries and deaths on the roads, the effects of increasing greenhouse gases on the climate, the bill is far nearer £53 billion. We are all of us, in other words, subsidising the drivers on the roads.

Like all taxes, green taxes are not popular. But everyone understands the sense in them, and - for good political reasons - it's sensible to cut other taxes. But green ones do have another

# orporate subsidies

## fare for the richest

nual total of perverse subsidies is
han all but the five leading national
ies, larger than the top 12
tions' annual sales, and... twice as
annual global military
g."
Myers, Royal Society of
re, 2000

es are a step in the right
but they are a drop in
compared to the taxes
subsidise activities then
eople and planet. While our
m to be working for sustainability,
mic system does the opposite. Who is
all this terrifying damage to the planet?
There are hidden health or environmental
esult, and these have to be paid for too.
mes, like the medical costs of increased
're not paid for properly.

Sometimes the real costs to future generations is
impossible to calculate. Like the future effects of
encouraging traffic by building roads, or encouraging
air travel by building runways and giving tax breaks
for air fuel. Or the long-term effects of subsidising
nuclear energy. Or the long-term effects
on children of encouraging a global
culture of Disney, McDonalds and
high-pressure marketing.

For example, how much of the £54
billion  health bill in the UK is a
direct result of the £5.5 billion a year
spent by the Goverment on road
transport? We don't know. But Prof Robin
Maynard said that about one in 50 heart attacks in
London is a direct result of traffic pollution.

The Campaign Against the Arms Trade reckons
that about £1.5 billion in taxpayers' money goes
into subsidising the arms trade, including the

problem: they are designed both to raise money
and to reduce pollution, so you can't entirely
predict their effects. The more effective they are
in persuading people not to drive or to smoke,
the less money they will yield - as has happened
with the London congestion charge.

But bundled together they are more predictable;
future taxes could include:

**Land:** land taxes – on site value – would reduce wasted
land. (They nearly became law in the UK twice, in 1915
and 1931.) Now they could raise about £50 billion a
year in the UK alone – though, by encouraging
development, land taxes might make cities less green.

**Rubbish:** the government's landfill tax is underpinned
by the European Union, which will fine the UK £500,000
if it misses targets for reducing rubbish dumping.

**Durability:** toasters, tumble dryers and even the kettles
in kitchens across Europe may cost more as a new law
forces manufacturers to pay for the recycling of their
products. About five million perfectly good computers
are currently put in landfill in the UK every year.

**Plastic bags:** the recent Irish tax of 10p per plastic
carrier bag has cut their use by over 90%.

**Energy:** the so-called Unitax – a single tax that
replaces all others on energy at the point of sale – has
been proposed as the most effective and least
avoidable tax. No sign of it yet, though.

**Out of town parking:** out of town superstores have
the benefit over town centres of letting people park for
free. A tax on each parking space would even up the
balance. (British superstores recently fought off such a
proposed tax.)

**Currency speculation:** the proposal by the Nobel
prize-winning economist James Tobin for a levy of
0.05% on speculative currency flows (see p 133) might
be the only way of raising enough for the UN to
implement its sustainable development ambitions.

*David Pearce and Edward B. Barbier*
*Blueprint for a Sustainable Economy*
Earthscan, 2000
ISBN 185383515

# Cost-benefit analysis

## Knowing the price of everything

Measuring the costs or benefits of some of the side-effects of money – on health or the environment – is vital if you want to persuade people how they are damaging the planet. To convince people that taxing aviation fuel (currently exempt) is a good idea, you need to calculate the real costs of flying: the pollution, the concrete, the road traffic, the greenhouse effect and much more.

*"A man who knows the price of everything and the value of nothing."*
Oscar Wilde's definition of a cynic

But there are problems in calculating the price of health or the environment. Cost-benefit analysis began as a way for French railway engineers to work out what to charge for railway tickets on new lines, and was developed by the US Army Corps of Engineers as a way to take the politics out of dam-building decisions. It became part of the modern fantasy that somehow decisions can be made 'scientifically' by technocrats, without recourse to old-fashioned discussion.

The biggest cost-benefit analysis ever was carried out in the late 1960s to work out where to build the third London Airport. Critics said that, if you really took such calculations seriously, it would be cheaper to build it in Hyde Park, but Westminster Abbey would have to be demolished. (A retired air marshal wrote to the *Daily Telegraph* to say he had been arguing the Hyde Park case for years!).

During this process, economists valued the medieval church at Cublington at £51,000 if demolished.

Modern cost-benefit analysis uses the amount of money people are willing to pay to save whales or the Grand Canyon, for example. The idea is to find some basis for international negotiations, but the danger is that economists might really believe the price is real – because, of course, such things as species, life, beauty are actually priceless.

Still, economists worked out that all elephants are worth $100 million, or that the Grand Canyon is worth $4.43 per person per month, or that an American life was worth 15 times more than a Chinese life. The danger was that these prices could seep out of political negotiations and onto people's balance sheets.

Already the world economy values an Albanian orphan at £4,000 and a reasonably sized house in central London at over £1 million. People really believe these things.

And you can't really measure willingness to pay. About a quarter of people asked what they would be willing to pay to preserve bald eagles, woodpeckers, coyotes, salmon or wild turkeys refuse to reply on

*Blueprin*

the grounds that you can'
things. And of course you c:
called Frau Kraus discovered
veto over a proposed new sl
build next door, and refusec
She turned down a mi
she turned dowr
they were
wou
tc
b
s

decisions. But it is a us
'true' costs of unsusta

C

Wel

*"The ar
larger t
econon
corporc
large a:
spendin
Norman
Arts lect

Green tax
direction,
the ocean
we pay to
damage p
leaders cla
the econo
paying for
We all are.
costs as a
And somet
traffic, they

Defence Export Services Organisation and subsidies for arms exports via the Export Credit Guarantee scheme.

Then there's food. According to Prof. Jules Pretty, externalities in agriculture mean we pay for our food three times over – once in the shops, once as taxpayers for the subsidy and once as taxpayers to clean up some of the mess from the way it's done. The situation is even worse elsewhere:

**Pesticides**: subsidies paid by EU taxpayers under the Common Agricultural Policy go towards the 22 million kilos of pesticide used in UK agriculture every year. The big food conglomerates are 'subsidised' because they don't pay the full costs of damage from road transport.

**Energy**: Western European governments are subsidising energy to the tune of about £9 billion – 63% of it for fossil fuels, 28% for nuclear energy and a measly 9% for renewables. (The renewables subsidies include backing for incinerators that take the pressure off local government to make recycling work.)

**Fossil fuels**: Germany subsidises mining by about £11,000 per miner per year: it would be more efficient to send all their miners home on full pay – and thus cut greenhouse emissions.

**Fisheries**: ocean fisheries cost more than £66 billion a year, but the fish are sold for about £48 billion. The worldwide shortfall is funded by governments, which thus contribute to making commercial fishing almost extinct.

Corporate subsidies worldwide total around £1,200 billion, in a global economy worth £18,000 billion, mainly to support agriculture, fossil fuels, nuclear energy, road transport, water and fisheries. There are 40,000 lobbyists in Brussels alone, making sure this corporate featherbedding continues.

*World Bank support for transport:*
| | |
|---|---|
| *Roads* | *98%* |
| *Rail* | *2%* |

Norman Myers and Jennifer Kent
*Perverse Subsidies: How misused tax dollars harm the environment and the economy*
Island Press, 2001
ISBN 1559638354

Section IV

# Debt money

Where did all the money go? There's enough to create tidal waves around the world financial system, but not enough – it seems – for the important things in life, such as small shops and healthy food or local buses and local police. Why is this? It may have something to do with debt...

# The hidden flaw in money

## The trouble with interest

There's something miraculous about modern money: it seems to grow all by itself.

Certainly, compound interest is miraculous if you're on the right side of it. It makes pensions possible. It means we no longer have workhouses. And it gives us a warm feeling inside as we watch the money in our building society slowly breed.

*"It is amazing that this monster interest has not devoured the whole of humanity. It would have done so long ago had not bankruptcy and revolution acted as counter-poisons."*
Napoleon Bonaparte

But if we're in debt, the idea of interest isn't quite so comfortable. Like Third World nations, every time we look at our debt bill it seems even bigger. The existence of interest is wonderful for people with money, and a burden for those without. That's only one reason to be suspicious of it.

It's unnatural for money to make money out of money. The ancient Egyptians had a money system that worked the other way round. They would put their grain in a barn in exchange for wooden tally sticks, then they used the sticks as money. But while they did so, the value of their savings wouldn't increase, as ours does. Quite the reverse – the rats would eat it and it would go mouldy, and as time passed, it would be worth less than it was before. Nobody would suggest going back to tally sticks, but that's what happens when money is based on something real (see p 141).

Most major religions condemn 'usury', though Christianity and Judaism centuries ago allowed a reasonable percentage. But Islam sticks to the original interpretation.

It has a point. According to the German architect Margrit Kennedy, a penny invested at average rates of interest at the time of Christ would now be worth nearly 9,000 balls of gold, each equal to the weight of the earth. "The economic necessity and the mathematical impossibility create a contradiction ...which has led to innumerable feuds, wars and revolutions in the past," she wrote. That's the danger of charging interest.

Since most money in circulation is created via loans from banks (see page 16), then nearly all money – except the notes and coins in our pockets – carries this burden as it has to be paid back some day, plus interest. Nature isn't like that: it doesn't grow nearly so fast.

"The assumption is that growth is good and more is better," said the green economist Paul Ekins. "It's as if economists have never heard of cancer." So why does modern economics insist that countries and businesses grow so maniacally? Interest is probably the culprit. It has to grow just to afford the interest repayments on debt. That's why business has to create 'need' by high-pressure marketing. The world can no longer stand still.

Strangely, one of the fastest growing sectors of financial services is based on Islamic principles and refuses to charge interest. There are now more than 200 Islamic financial institutions spread across the Middle East, with more in the Far East, with assets of around $200 billion. Even HSBC and Citibank have opened Islamic operations in the Persian Gulf, and HSBC offers Islamic mortgages in New York. Islamic banks don't charge interest when they lend money, but take part ownership instead. So money invested in an Islamic bank keeps 'working'. If they invest in a weak business then they may lose money.

The success of the Scandinavian interest-free bank JAK implies the same thing: it may be that interest-free money represents the future.

> *The Triodos Bank in Bristol only lends 'ethically' and pays low interest to savers. Yet it is booming.*

Margrit Kennedy, with Declan Kennedy
*Interest and Inflation Free Money*
New Society, 1996
ISBN 0865713103

# Mortgages

## The death grip

*"Slavery they can have anywhere. It is a weed that grows in every soil."*
Edmund Burke, 1775

When people complain that dinner party conversation is obsessed with the value of people's homes, we assume that staying glued to the window of the estate agents - watching their prices rise or fall - somehow means being obsessed with trivia. And it is, in a sense. But in another sense, house prices and the mortgages that drive them are more important than we often realise. And here are three reasons why:

They are not based on real values. The extraordinary rise in house prices in Britain - from an average UK price of £5,000 in 1970 to around £120,000 today - has led to a massive shift in value from one generation to the next. Thousands of ordinary people become millionaires simply from the sale of their parents' homes. But when houses are used as security for other loans, we should beware, because house prices are not real. My small house is, apparently, worth far more than would actually be needed to rebuild it.

> *"Consumers have obliged central bankers and economists by joining the money merry-go-round, borrowing heavily and then propping up economies with their spending. When the music stops, these consumers will be heavily indebted and badly hurt."*
> Ann Pettifor, *Real World Economic Outlook*

They force up house prices. House prices are supposed to rise because of supply and demand, and - now that London homes are increasingly used as investments - that's partly true. But the real supply driving the price of homes is money: the amount mortgage lenders are prepared to pay. Tokyo house prices multiplied ten times over in the 1980s because 'grandparent mortgages' were invented, whereby the money would be paid off in two generations' time.

**We need mortgages more than we know:** As much as two thirds of the money in circulation in Britain was created as mortgage loans. If we didn't have high house prices - under current arrangements at least - our money would dry up.

**We can never pay them off:** It may be possible for us individually to pay off our mortgages, but as a community we never will - partly because the nation needs the money in circulation (see left), and partly because there may not be enough money in circulation to pay it off. We have debts of over £800 billion in the UK, and only around $700 billion in circulation.

The word mortgage means 'death grip' or 'death promise' and used to be a last resort method of raising money, using your property as collateral. Even in the early years of widespread home ownership in the 1930s, with affordable semi-detached houses widely available, most mortgages were for 15 years and took less than a tenth of your salary. They were also usually paid off early.

These days, mortgage payments can take up well over a third of our income, and we can only afford houses in the first place if two people are earning to pay it off. About 37% of the UK housing stock is mortgaged, and it is more and more difficult to get on the bottom rung of the housing ladder.

It is a strange paradox that the houses were built and paid for long ago, yet we own fewer and fewer of them as time goes by. Why should a third of all Britain's housing stock be owned by the mortgage lenders? And every time financial institutions lend more, they are feeding the continuing house price spiral in a self-defeating vicious circle that cannot continue for ever.

### The rise of mortgages

1930 2x annual salary, and 8% of annual income
2000 4x annual salary, and 20% of annual income

Michael Rowbotham
*The Grip of Death: A study of modern money, debt slavery and destructive economics*
Jon Carpenter, 1998
ISBN 1897766408

# Debt 1

## Weighing down the world

Nearly all the money in circulation is there because it was borrowed, and that means that we are struggling under a monstrous weight of debt. That's true for us as individuals, as companies and as nations.

Corporations need to be seriously indebted just to protect themselves from hostile takeovers. If they have spare borrowing capacity, the chances are that a corporate raider could use it to issue junk bonds with which to buy the company (see p 127). Then they are forced into ever more ambitious expansion plans just to pay off the interest on their loans. Japanese banks alone have over $800 billion in bad loans on their books. This threatens to bring down, not just the edifice of the Japanese economy, but other economies as well.

One of the reasons why corporations are so fragile - only three of the names from the Fortune 500 list half a century ago have managed to survive - is this weight of debt.

As individuals, our unused capacity to borrow is the subject of serious marketing pressure. In the USA, credit card companies even market themselves by sending cheques for $5,000 through the post. The average American has been offered 32 credit cards regardless of their credit history. All you have to do to open an account and spend the money is fill in your name - "like feeding lettuce to hungry rabbits", according to one commentator.

For those who are too bad a credit risk to be able to borrow from the banks, there are the loan sharks and money lenders, offering loans at outrageous rates of interest - even sometimes up to 5,000% APR (see p 23). It isn't surprising that 4% of UK credit cards have more than £5,000 in debt on them – which will take a decade to pay off if you pay the minimum, and cost the same again in interest.

US consumer debt has reached an all-time high of over $1,000 billion, and credit card debts account for approximately $400 billion of that.

But most frightening of all is the weight of debt that is impoverishing people's lives in developing countries, often lent by western banks to ferocious military regimes that have since disappeared. As much as $1,700 billion is now outstanding - all but $400 billion of it the result of mounting compound interest. The countries of Sub-Saharan Africa pay $10 billion every year in debt service, or about four times as much money as the countries in the region spend on health care and education.

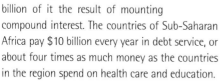

This all has to be repaid, not in their own currencies, but in pounds or dollars, which they can only earn by converting forests or marginal land to grow cash crops for export like coffee - the value of which, like other commodities, has fallen for a generation. But it's worse than that:

• The trickle of aid money that goes from the rich north to the poor south is dwarfed by their enormous daily interest payments back again. For every pound spent on aid by OECD countries, £10 is sent back by poor countries in debt repayments, money that should have been spent on health and education.

• Even after the promises and hype, only 20% of the debt of the 42 poorest countries has been cancelled. Much of it is still unrepayable and blights the lives of the poorest people in the world.

• International loans are negotiated in secret between local elites and the powerful creditors – but the effects are felt by ordinary people.

• As much as 95% of debts owed to Britain are owed to the government's Export Credit Guarantee Department as inducements to buy British exports – mainly arms.

• There is no international bankruptcy law to protect debtors and no international receiver: creditors are judge and jury in their own court.

## But then, who really owes whom?

**Eco-debt:** damage to the planet's eco-system is done by rich countries, but has its greatest effect on poor countries: 96% of deaths from natural disasters are in poor countries, and seven million people are at risk from rising sea levels.

**Imperial debt:** in the 150 years after Columbus, 185,000 kilos of gold and 16 million kilos of silver were taken from Central America to Europe. Was it theft or just a loan?

**Historic debt:** in 1193, England agreed to pay Germany £66,000 in silver – then a quarter of their GDP – to ransom Richard the Lionheart. It has never been completely paid. Some debts do get overtaken by history – or should that one be repaid too?

Some countries, of course, manage loans better than others - and the right to credit is important - but the lender should be equally responsible for the original loan.

*Average household debt in the UK:*
*1997            £24,500*
*2003            £37,500*
*Source: office for National Statistics*

*The World Bank and IMF forced Malawi to sell 28,000 tons of maize stocks to pay dollar debts in 2002. Three months later, the population was facing starvation.*

www.jubileeplus.org

# Debt 2

## Weighing down the USA

*"280 million Americans bingeing on Toyota Land Cruisers, Sony video players and Cartier watches - are doing so by raiding the piggy bank savings of five billion people in developing countries. It's time the rich financed the poor, instead of filching from them."*
Ann Pettifor, *Jubilee Research*

Round the corner from Times Square in New York City there is a rapidly spinning counter that reveals how much the USA is in debt. It is now running at $6,467,436,375,130 and seven cents, which means over $22,000 per person – and increasing at the rate of $1.35 billion a day, even before the Iraq war.

Local government in the USA has also been on a spending binge and now owes so much that it is paying $358 billion in interest payments - more than they are paying on parks, libraries and recreation combined - and all to be paid off by later generations.

The USA used to be the world's creditor nation, forcing the British to restructure their economy after the First World War - and it is a creditor to many of the poorest countries in the world. But it is also now massively in debt itself to the rest of the world.

Every day, the US government finances itself by selling Treasury bonds and Treasury bills, paying a set amount of interest, to whoever has money to lend. When the bonds and bills become due, it borrows more to pay them, as well as to pay the cost of arms, tax cuts and all the rest of their unsustainable budget, which ballooned in the presidency of Ronald Reagan. Its budgets were balanced again in the Clinton years but unbalanced again by George W. Bush's tax cuts and military adventures. The effect is to hoover up most of the available money in the world.

Ironically, it is the savers, pension funds and central banks of the poorer countries in the world, as well as countries with a trade surplus - like France, Germany and the Far East - who keep the money flowing. The world trusts the US to pay its debts, and no creditor so far has dared demand that America restructure itself.

Experts are divided about what this means: can it just continue or will there be some bizarre crack in the world's financial architecture? Nobody knows, but the ironies are very peculiar:

- The USA alone owes almost as much as the whole developing world put together (about $2,500 billion), including India, China and Brazil.
- It also pays only $20 billion a year to service its debt, while poor countries are crippled by more than $300 billion servicing the same amount, because they are considered to be greater risks.
- Poor countries borrow funds from the USA at rates as high as 18% interest a year while at the same time lending to the USA at rates as low as just 3%.
- This means the developing world is actually financing the massive deficits of the USA, partly because of the hoover effect and partly because their central banks are forced to hold dollar reserves as insurance against speculation and financial instability.

But then, who knows, the poorest nations may yet wake up to their unexpectedly powerful position. The fear is that forcing the USA to restructure its debts could have devastating consequences for the rest of the world.

*US Trade Deficit:*

| | |
|---|---|
| *2000* | *$400 billion* |
| *2002* | *$500 billion* |
| *2004* | *$700 billion\** |
| | *\*predicted* |

*The Real World Economic Outlook: The Legacy of Globalization: Debt and Deflation*
(editor) Ann Pettifor
Palgrave Macmillan, 2003
ISBN 1403917957

# Where has all the money gone?

## The problem with modern money

*"The plain fact is that a man, and his wife, and with four children that are unable to work, cannot now, out of his labour, possibly provide them and himself with the means for living... And will anyone say that this state of things is such as England ought to witness?"*
William Cobbett

My parents live in a little village called Nether Wallop. A generation ago it had two shops, a post office, two pubs, a butcher, a policeman, a doctor and district nurse, and a nearby railway station – connected to a massive local rail network.

And that was in the Austerity years of the 1940s. Now, when we are incomparably 'richer', all that's left is one pub and a very occasional bus. The conventional reasons for this – low taxes, over-regulation, fat-cat salaries – don't really explain why it's so hard to afford the simplest public services, health, post and education any more, or basic shops. And when we're so wealthy too.

Policy-makers have their noses glued to the short-term, and they find it hard to ask long-term questions. But an increasingly urgent question is: why can we only afford a creaking postal delivery system that occasionally delivers letters within 24 hours, and barely adequate railways? Or why - for example - do restaurants

have to be almost fully booked just to avoid bankruptcy? Why can't we afford to clean the streets or get the litter out of the parks? Why can we not afford full care for the mentally ill?

Victorian economists worked out that in 1495, peasants had to work at least 15 weeks a year to earn the money they needed to survive. By 1564 it was 40 weeks. Now it is impossible for one person on average wages to buy a home in south east England and live reasonably in it: that requires two salaries.

The 20th-century predictions that we would all soon relax into a leisured life, fuelled by technology and the effects of compound interest, have not come true. Some flaw in the economic system has conspired to turn us instead into slaves to our mortgages.

Why does the system work like that? There is no definitive answer, and most economists don't even ask the question, but here are some possible reasons:

**Burgeoning debt**: at least a third of the price of the goods we pay, or the rooms we rent, goes on interest payments to cover the money borrowed. An average 28% of the income of UK business goes to service their debt.

**Offshore tax havens**: between a sixth and a third of the world's wealth is now hidden offshore to avoid tax (see p 52).

**The curse of the middlemen**: half a century ago, American farmers used to get 41 cents of every dollar spent on the food they grew. Now they get just 9 cents, with 24 cents going on seeds, energy, fertiliser and other inputs, and 67 cents going to marketeers, middlemen, transport and supermarkets.

**Intellectual property**: the ultra-rich now siphon off much of the available money in the world, through interest payments, copyrights or intellectual property or rents - taking rights over other people's money, media, manufactures or homes (see p 54).

**Monopolies**: just 13 big bread manufacturers now control a £3 billion industry producing airy nothingness with so little in it that it has to be injected with vitamins. It's the same in so many other industries.

Whatever the reason, the trend is clear: we are turning ourselves into economic slaves - and creating a world where the public 'good' seems more and more unaffordable. What can we do about it?

We can find new ways of creating a range of new kinds of money that are locally controlled (see p 52). We can persuade the government to start issuing its own interest-free money - put into circulation, rather than borrowed into existence with interest attached, as it usually is (see page 138).

We can also limit the ownership rights of investors. If investors never look beyond 20 years when they buy foreign companies or build foreign factories - and they don't - then we are overpaying them by giving them perpetual rights. The Australian thinker and former financier, Shann Turnbull, suggests that rights should revert to locals after one generation (see p 56).

But most of all, we should be aware of what is happening. Ordinary people are increasingly indebted, public bodies are increasingly cash-strapped, and governments are increasingly penniless. Corporations are increasingly wealthy, but so dependent on the tyranny of the stock markets and their own share price that they dare not step out of line. Between them, the money that allows us to live is being allowed to slip away.)

*The Money Changers:*
*Currency reform from Aristotle to e-cash*
David Boyle (editor)
Earthscan, 2002
1 85383 895 0

# Pensions

## One thing after another

*"This was a massive debacle. We just hope it never happens again."*
Malcolm McLean, UK Pensions Advisory Service on the latest pensions scandal.

A century ago or more, music hall audiences would dab their eyes at the end of the song *My Old Dutch* - "we've been together now for 40 years/ And it don't seem a day too much" - watching the elderly couple separate forever into the Men and Women's entrances of the workhouse.

We don't have to face that prospect any more, partly because of state pensions, introduced by David Lloyd George in his People's Budget of 1909, which finally swept away the workhouses before the First World War. And partly because of the effects of compound interest - the 'original sin' at the heart of the money system - which allows people to build up enough savings to see them through their retirement. There was

a time when employees would pay regularly into their company pension scheme every week, and - thanks to the magical effects of compound interest - they would be rewarded with maybe three decades of happy workhouse-free retirement.

But that has all begun to unravel. This is partly because of the unsustainable effects of endless money growth – the planet doesn't work like that (see p 86) – and partly, of course, the simultaneous collapse of the stock market and interest rates. Also we have an ageing population and falling savings rates. So we are faced again with the return of the spectre of poverty-stricken old age, thanks to the mixture of incompetence, arrogance and corporate greed that has undermined confidence in financial services on both sides of the Atlantic.

Recent scandals include:

**The Savings and Loans Scandal:** when US building societies (savings and loans) were deregulated in the mid-1980s, and were allowed to lend their own owners money. The result was an explosion of greed, corruption and political slush-funds that amounted to the largest theft in the history of the world - implicating Republicans at the highest level - and will eventually cost the US government $1,400 billion. That's enough to provide pre-natal care for every American child for 2,300 years. The few who went to jail received sentences on average a fifth that of the average bank robber.

**The Maxwell Scandal:** when he fell off his yacht in the Bay of Biscay, the publishing tycoon Robert Maxwell turned out to have been plundering the pensions of his Mirror publishing group. Workers who saved for years have got reduced pensions as a result and, several years on, none of the highly paid professionals who were supposed to be taking responsibility for the security of the pension fund have been punished.

**The Pensions Mis-selling scandal:** up to two million UK customers were mis-sold personal pensions and pension top-ups, persuaded to opt-out of company schemes that would have been far more beneficial. The scandal looks set to cost insurers and financial advisers at least £11.8bn in compensation payments. The UK's financial services watchdog has taken disciplinary action against 346 firms.

**The Company Pensions Scandal:** most companies are backing off their commitments to look after staff in old age, with only four out of ten final-salary schemes still open to new members. They are being replaced by so-called 'money purchase' schemes, which do not guarantee a certain level of pension on retirement. They also cost the company less.

**The Privatisation Scandal:** the privatised National Bus Company was sold off by the Conservative government, which then allowed its pension fund surplus to be counted as an asset of the privatised company, benefiting shareholders rather than the staff who had paid for it.

**The Winding-up Scandal:** employees who had paid into company schemes for decades are finding themselves without pensions because of a decision by boards to wind their company up. Worse, they have to watch while up to 15% of some pension funds disappear into the pockets of lawyers, actuaries and professional trustees during the wind-up process.

What can we do about all this? For one thing, state pensions should, properly, be for a living income. And our private pension funds have got to find something more reliable to invest in than the global casino – such as safe and productive havens like local housing, transport or health projects (see p 178). We need to reconnect state pensions to average earnings. But we also need new ways of safeguarding ourselves in old age – making sure there is a supportive community around us to keep us healthy and at home, which is one of the reasons time banks were first introduced (see p 155).

Robin Blackburn
*Banking on Death: The uses and misuses of pension funds*
Verso, 2001
ISBN 1859847951

# Another way of making money 1

## Creating more cash

*"If the government can create a dollar bond, they can create a dollar bill."*
Henry Ford, *New York Times*, 1921

What can we do about the dwindling supply of money for some key sectors, cities and public projects? The problem, according to some, is that so much of the money in circulation is created by banks and based on debt that has to be paid back plus interest. The solution then is to get the central bank to issue interest-free money.

This was a popular radical solution in the mid-20th century, with the leading economist Irving Fisher urging a ban on banks from creating money. If they lent money they would have actually to use what had been deposited with them and nothing more.

One simple way, an idea that has recently been before Parliament and the US Congress, is for the Bank of England to issue money debt-free and lend it to pay for public infrastructure like new railways or hospitals - then take it out of circulation again when it's paid off. This was the solution proposed in 1921 by the industrialists Henry Ford and Thomas Alva Edison.

If the money has to be created anyway, it might be less inflationary if it was created by the government without interest than if it was created by the banks. Economists say that interest is a discipline on big loans and that's true. But it's an expensive discipline: investors in the London Underground expect to make about £2.7 billion over the life of the PPP (Public-Private Partnership), in return for investments of just £530 million - and a third of that will go to financial intermediaries.

There are precedents too:

**Bradburys**: in 1914, the Chancellor of the Exchequer, David Lloyd George, staved off a banking collapse by getting the Treasury to print their own bank notes, known as 'bradburys' because they were signed by the Treasury Secretary Sir John Bradbury. The banks were furious when it continued.

**Cash**: about 3% of the money in circulation is created in this way already - and it used to be much more. These are the notes and coins the government issues, making a profit known as 'seigniorage' – the difference between what it costs to print notes and their face value. This is known to economists as M0, as opposed to all those other measures of money in circulation, M1, M2, M3 etc.

**Cash again**: a while ago in 1960, about 21% of the money in circulation was issued by the Bank of England as cash - and inflation was the same as it is today. So there must be a scope to do the same now.

The government has the right to create the credit it needs for civilised investments, and should do so.

James Robertson and Joseph Huber
*Creating New Money: A monetary reform for the information age*
New Economics Foundation, 2000
ISBN 1899407294

# Another way of making money 2

## Social credit and the rise of the Greenshirts

*"Banking was conceived in iniquity and born in sin ... Bankers own the earth. Take it away from them but leave them the power to create money, and with a flick of the pen, they will create enough money to buy it back again."*
Sir Josiah Stamp, reforming Bank of England director

In the turbulent 1920s and 1930s, the idea of the government creating new money became the central belief of a new ideology - arising out of a strange amalgam of socialism and enthusiasm for the days of medieval guilds - known as social credit.

The problem is worse than we thought, according to its founder, 'Major' Clifford Hugh Douglas, an engineer at the Farnborough aircraft factories. There isn't enough money in circulation to pay off all the debts in the world, he said - and this is still so today - so our lives are bound to slip further and further into the control of the banks.

Douglas's 1920 book *Economic Democracy* caused a major division on the Left of politics, and - although it was never quite clear what he wanted to do about it - a powerful manifesto grew up around him. It included banning the banks from creating money altogether - so they could only lend what someone had deposited with them - and creating money in the form of a basic income for every citizen, credited to their account every month, which would 'trickle up' the economy rather than 'trickle down' as it was usually supposed to do.

By the 1930s, Douglas was able to command stadiums full of supporters in Australia and Canada, as well as in the UK. An estimated 90 million tuned into his radio broadcasts in the USA, and two Canadian states elected social credit administrations. They stayed in power in Alberta until 1971, prevented by the courts from pushing through their promised $25 dividend per person a month.

In the UK, a breakaway wing of the Boy Scouts formed itself into the Social Credit Party - much to Douglas's horror - and marched the streets as the Greenshirts. The extraordinary man behind it, John Hargrave, became a notorious figure just before the war when a green arrow was fired into the door of 10 Downing Street. But when he lost his deposit in Stoke Newington in the 1950 general election, he wound the party up.

Social credit petered out in anti-semitism and paranoia in the 1950s: for some reason, those who believe there is a conspiracy of bankers seem to be only a hair's-breadth away from believing it's a Jewish one. The conspiracies are still there on the internet: both Lincoln and Kennedy are supposed to have been assassinated because they were poised to take on the banks.

But Douglas influenced young economists like James Meade - who claimed Keynes had learned from him too. And now, half a century later, social credit has shaken off its anti-semitism and is back in vogue as a radical solution to the world debt crisis. But it is still controversial because of the plan to hand power over the money supply to the centre - whether it is the government or a few establishment figures around a table.

Governments have always been notorious for their uncertainty over how much money to issue, but even an 'independent' board is a centralising force. This is the stuff of radical debate: the present system doesn't work, but do we concentrate money-creating power at the centre or do we widen the number of institutions able to create money?

Personally, I would prefer to spread the ability to create the money we need as widely as possible. But social credit has a fascinating and neglected history, and Douglas very nearly succeeded in his campaign – and may do yet.

Frances Hutcheson
*What Everyone Wants to Know about Money*
Jon Carpenter, 1998
ISBN 1897766335

# Another way of making money 3

## A new global currency of oil, metal, food…

*"We have had no reality, no stability. The price of gold has risen by more than 70%. That is as if a 12-inch foot rule had suddenly stretched to 19 or 20 inches."* Winston Churchill, on his disastrous decision to return the pound to the gold standard

What can we do about the dwindling supply of money for some vital aspects of life? The problem, according to others, is that money has become a commodity in its own right. Because it isn't based on the value of anything, it can be worth whatever people in Wall Street say it is – and that really can be anything. There is always somewhere more profitable for it to be lodged than in growing anything or making anything.

In those circumstances, it isn't surprising that it slips effortlessly out of the hands of small farmers or manufacturers and into the hands of banks, hedge funds, financial services and the mega-rich.

That's what happens, they say, when the vast majority of money in the world is fiat money (see p 140): currencies which exist just because their governments say they exist, their value underpinned by debt – by what the governments borrowed to create it and by confidence in their ability to repay it.

But there is a long tradition that demands something different. They extend from the French

anarchist Pierre-Joseph Proudhon and his People's Bank, (see p 149) who wanted money based on the value of goods and services, to the American conscientious objector Bob Swann, who invented money based on farm produce (see p 146).

They include Keynes, whose plan for the economic system after World War II - rejected by the US government - included an international currency that would underpin everything else and was based on commodities like wheat or oil. This kind of stability was urgent during the post-war famine years in Europe: the grand old man of investment banking, Benjamin Graham, proposed a global currency based on the value of food kept in stores around the world.

Most recently, there has been the plan by one of the original designers of the euro, Bernard Lietaer, for the 'terra' – a world currency, based on a basket of commodities (anything from copper to sugar), that would keep all the other currencies stable. It would:

**Be inflation proof,** because its value would rise or fall with what oil, wheat or copper was really worth.

**Have a negative interest charge** (see p 141) to make it real - real commodities rust and go mouldy after all. This would also discourage speculators from hoarding it.

**Cool down the world's economy** in boom periods and kick-start it in recessions.

**Help anyone who produced commodities,** in the developing world, by cutting the costs of storage.

**Provide the world with a much-needed standard of value** to stop speculators having such power.

There's no sign of the 'terra' yet, but the arguments for it remain as relevant as ever - not instead of other currencies, national and local, but to complement and support them.

Bernard Lietaer
*The Future of Money: A new way to create wealth, work and a wiser world*
Century, 2001
ISBN 0712699910

# Citizens' income

## The right to life

*"A feast is made for laughter, and wine maketh merry; but money answereth all things."*
Ecclesiastes 10:19

Vast bureaucracies spend enormous sums of money every year trying to make sure that nobody gets unemployment benefits, or any other kind of pay-out, unless they really need them. You can't help wondering whether it would be cheaper just to give them to everyone.

When you think how easy it is to earn a living doing jobs of no possible use to people or planet (like writing tobacco adverts, flipping hamburgers for McDonalds), and how difficult it is to get paid to do jobs that aren't valued in the market (childcare, looking after the environment), you have to wonder whether it might be better to cut the link between jobs and basic income altogether.

People could then earn extra money for luxuries, but – if they wanted just to devote their life to art, or looking after their elderly parents – they could do so.

That was one of the ideas behind the social credit movement in the 1930s (see p 102), though the social credit government in Alberta in 1935 was prevented by the Canadian supreme court from paying everyone a 'dividend' every month. A minority report to the Beveridge plan for the welfare state in 1943 proposed something similar, but paid for out of taxation. The idea of tax credits for families is also a slow movement towards a basic citizen's income – making sure that every individual has enough to live on – but it isn't there yet. The idea still has some way to go before it is accepted widely - partly because of the rise in taxes that would be needed to pay for a citizen's income high enough.

Opinions differ about what it would cost. There are other pitfalls too: employers would be tempted to lower wages, knowing that the state was taking over their responsibility. It might lower some people's self-esteem, because they wouldn't be forced to go out to earn – and that can be a life-saver for some people. But even so, the benefits of a citizen's income could be enormous. It would mean, for example:

• No more means testing, no more bullying unemployment benefits officials, no vast welfare bureaucracy, because everyone would have the means to live on – as of right.

• No more trapping artists, actors, poets and others in inappropriate jobs just to make ends meet.

• No more chasing after the very people who keep neighbourhoods running - spending their time looking out for people, supporting the elderly, building social capital - to force them out to look for 'paid' work.

• No more of the nonsense where people can be paid to look after the children next door, but not for looking after their own.

There may be other ways to pay for the citizens' income too. Norway invests its oil revenues into a fund that will benefit future generations. And if foreign investments reverted to local ownership after 20 years (see p 56), people could be paid an annual dividend every year from the profits.

People who play important but 'non-economic' roles in society may not deserve vast hand-outs from the state, but they do deserve the basic necessities (see p 156). The current system now defines what a job is more and more narrowly, and it may impoverish us all by driving out everything that isn't immediately marketable. Unless we have citizens' incomes, of course.

www.citizensincome.org

# Micro-credit

## Small banking is beautiful

The Bangladeshi economics professor Mohammed Yunus was at a conference of New York bankers in 1976 when he realised that at least 80% of his countrymen would be turned down for loans by those in the room.

He went home and founded the Grameen Bank, now the model for micro-lending and small-scale banking all over the world. It lends very small amounts – enough for a hen or a cow, or, more recently, a mobile phone that can be used by a whole village ("a mobile phone is a cow," they say at Grameen). The money is lent almost entirely to women, because they were found to manage money better than men, and each loan is rooted in support groups of other women.

*"The question isn't whether people are credit-worthy. It is, whether banks are people-worthy?"*
Mohammed Yunus, founder of Grameen Bank

Grameen operated originally from motor-scooters, around some of the poorest villages in the world.

"Your bank just rushed past in a cloud of dust," said the headline of the first article about them in *Christian Science Monitor*.

It was also enormously successful. Not only did they reduce bad debts to just 1% – compared to 10% for western banks lending to rich people – they also set out a whole new model of development that could genuinely help the poorest people stay independent. They now have a presence in 35,000 villages, with 12,000 workers and two million borrowers – 94% of whom are women – and they have serious political clout

Grameen also allows people to find the investment they need to make a major difference to people's lives, by providing services or food neighbours in the poorest places – rather than waiting hopelessly for big corporations to provide anything along the same lines.

It has spawned thousands of micro-credit projects all over the world, one of the ways that the First World is learning about development from the Third World. Micro-credit reached its apotheosis with the UN Micro-Credit summit in 1996, hosted in Washington by Hillary Clinton. Similar ideas have worked well in many other countries including Poland, and the Polish model – Fundusz Mikro, the creation of British merchant banker Rosalind Copisarow – is now working well in Britain. Some of the other models include:

**Grameenphone**: providing phone services in Bangladesh where they are otherwise non-existent. (Bangladeshis who want a mobile have to wait ten years and pay $500, whereas New Yorkers can get one immediately, free and over the counter.)

**Credit unions**: the small community-controlled savings and loan schemes that have spread from Ireland to the UK, giving poorest people some financial clout; they otherwise have to rely on loan sharks charging up to 5,000% APR.

**Social banks**: like the London Rebuilding Society, the Aston Reinvestment, the Triodos Bank in Bristol (and Spain and Holland) and the famous South Shore Bank in Chicago, that lend money to social enterprises – profit-making companies with social objectives – providing services to inner city areas.

Mohammad Yunus
*Banker to the Poor:*
*The story of the Grameen Bank*
Aurum Press, 2003
ISBN 1854109243

Section V

# Mad money

The world's financial system creates new billionaires every day, presides over grinding poverty and debt, and is increasingly unstable – and among the people who run it are 24-year-olds in braces in London and New York who make more money the more it fluctuates. It's a crazy world out there…

# Criminal money

## The shadow economy

*"I am just a businessman."*
Al Capone

One of the peculiar attributes of money is that, throughout history, it has tended to drive out entrenched privilege. Medieval rulers watched in horror as merchants affected equality with them simply because they had money. So they hurriedly rushed through rules about what people of different classes could wear, even banning non-aristocrats from playing chess (and possibly winning). But it all got swept away: that was the power of money. It has an aristocracy of its own, but it destroys any other.

But with social privilege made porous, money now devours anything that gets in the way – family, morality, community, laws – with terrifying rapidity. The result is that the biggest industries in the world, apart from oil and arms, are now drugs, sex and illegal immigration.

The annual profits from drug trafficking (cannabis, cocaine, heroin) are estimated at $300-$500 billion, which is getting on for 10% of all world trade. Even software piracy has a turnover of more than $200 billion, with counterfeit goods – all those pirated CDs and videos – at around $100 billion. The more copyrights and patents spread, the more delighted the 'underworld' will be.

The annual, world turnover of crime in the world every year – the Gross Criminal Product – is now believed to run at around $1,000 billion, or about 20% of world trade. Of that, about $350 billion is laundered through offshore financial centres and reinvested annually, at the rate of $1 billion a day.

Crime is very big business indeed. The world's largest outfit is the Hong Kong-based triad Sun Yee On, which employs between 47,000 and 60,000 members worldwide.

Compare that to the semi-legal arms trade, much of it subsidised by respectable governments. For example, the British export trade guarantees make up much of the Third World debt owed to the UK – about $800 billion a year.

Some of the activities of legitimate corporations could be included in the criminal class. Except when companies cause actionable damage – children born deformed because of chemicals used to grow tobacco, for example – these are known simply as 'externalities'. About 56,000 Americans die every year at work or from occupational diseases such as black lung and asbestosis. Hundreds of thousands of people all over the world also succumb to the silent violence of pollution, contaminated foods, hazardous consumer products, and hospital malpractice.

The top two companies with 'criminal records' in the 1990s were:

• Swiss drugs firm Hoffmann-La Roche, fined $500 million under international antitrust regulations.

• Japanese bank Daiwa, fined $340 million for involvement in money-laundering.

• Exxon Corporation and Exxon Shipping were also fined $125 million for pollution.

When business considers its only moral duty is to make a profit, what can we expect? (The charges against executives for inflating balance sheets and for the eventual collapse of Enron and WorldCom are just starting to emerge).

Nor is executive pay always quite the shadowy but wholly legal business it seems. The CEO of the US conglomerate Tyco, Dennis Kozlowski, and his finance chief Mark Swartz, were charged in 2003 with pilfering $400 million from company coffers over ten years. (He had a penchant for $6,000 shower curtains and $15,000 umbrella stands.)

# The curse of oil

## Why nothing is real any more

*"The Stone Age came to an end not for a lack of stones; the oil age will end, but not for a lack of oil."*
Sheik Yamani, the former oil minister of Saudi Arabia

"What makes her poor is her wealth," said a 16th-century Spanish economist about Spain, awash with gold and struggling with the effects of crippling inflation as a result. A similar disaster overtook Peru during the guano boom and Brazil during the rubber boom. These paradoxes are the basis for the so-called 'curse of oil'.

Nothing excites governments more than suddenly discovering, as the British did in the 1960s, that they have oil. The rush of black gold from the seabed or deep in the earth is enough to make the owners of the rights believe that their troubles are over once and for all. Actually the opposite is true, which is why the former

Venezuelan oil minister and co-founder of the petroleum-producing club OPEC called oil 'the devil's excrement'.

There are exceptions to the rule, like Norway and Malaysia which have used their oil revenues to diversify their economies, but generally speaking the countries that are most dependent on oil wealth do worse over time, and the countries least dependent on it do best. Strange isn't it.

Why should that be? What comes easy also goes easy: booms end (see p 129), leaving behind some gaudy buildings crumbling away, or ghost towns – all that's left of the gold rushes in California and Alaska. Meanwhile, the brief cascade of money has encouraged the beneficiaries to spend, spend, spend without much thought for the future – which always turns up in the end. Booms also drive out the most useful people. And if you doubt it, have a look at the small town of

Black Hawk after the legalisation of gambling in Colorado, where almost every public building has become a casino or slot machine arcade, and the only people on the streets are men in dark glasses offering to park your car. A similar process is under way on a grander scale in offshore financial centres (see p 52) like Jersey or Cyprus.

Oil lulls nations into a false sense of security. They believe the wealth will cushion them against the need for tough decisions and investment, and people still refuse to accept the tough decisions anyway. They believe energy will always be cheap – the same belief is crippling the USA – which means they never have to innovate to save energy. Meanwhile the inventions and efficiency that result from a shortage of energy go to their oil-poor competitors.

The UK's own version of the curse of oil affects other countries too: oil wealth feeds into wages and prices, and – worst of all – boosts the value of your currency in world markets as speculators buy into it for a while. Eventual result: people around the world can't afford your products, and your factories start closing one by one.

That's the curse of oil: all your economy is left with is oil and financial services. Manufacturing gets priced out, and anyway, why start a business – with all that effort and those low margins – when you can simply share in the spoils of the stock market bubbles? That's the trouble with successful modern economies: the real things suffer and get priced out by the unreal.

Terry Lynn Karl
*The Paradox of Plenty:*
*Oil booms and petro-states*
University of California Press, 1997
ISBN 0520207726

# Goodbye real world

## Money as a commodity

*"While a bushel of corn sold for less than $4, a bushel of corn flakes sold for $133."*
Canadian National Farmers Union report, 2000

About two centuries have gone by since the Industrial Revolution, and more than half a century since policy-makers started staring at the dial that showed economic 'growth' – but one thing never changes. No matter how much success the economy seems to produce, no matter how much production, the gulf between the rich and poor tends to remain – and grow.

When the shipping magnate Charles Booth organised the first door-to-door survey of London in the 1880s, to win a bet, he discovered that 30.5% of Londoners were 'poor'. Even further back, before the introduction of workhouses with the New Poor Law Amendment Act of 1834, just over 20% of national income in the UK was spent on welfare – handed out via the parishes.

Now in the 21st century, we measure these things differently, but both have remained broadly the same: about a third of our cities are poor, just as a third of nations are considered 'Less Developed Countries'.

But it's now more complicated than that – and worse. Money favours the already rich over the poor, and already rich places over poor countries. The unreal economy of financial services also favours speculation over the people who make things, just as it favours the people who know things over the people who grow things (see p 89). It also favours hard-edged pseudo-scientific skills – such as accountancy – over human skills like nursing.

Of all the money insanities in history, this is the most insidious, the most damaging and the most unfair. Why does it happen?

One clue is in the 2000 Canadian National Farmers union report: "While the farmers growing cereal grains are pushed close to bankruptcy, the companies that make breakfast cereals reap huge profits. In 1998, cereal companies Kellogg, Quaker Oats and General Mills enjoyed return on equity rates of 56%, 165% and 222% respectively. While a bushel of corn sold for less than $4, a bushel of corn flakes sold for $133. In 1998, the cereal companies were 186 to 740 times more profitable than the farms. Maybe farmers are making too little because others are taking too much."

The problem is the four Ms:

**Monopolies**: some big corporations are in a semi-monopolistic position, and they squeeze those who are unfortunate enough to rely on them – and are rewarded with a higher share price when they do – and none more so than the small farmers who are the backbone of any country's real production.

**Middlemen**: middlemen siphon off the money: manufacturers, in particular, have lost out to powerful intermediaries – supermarkets, marketeers, advertisers. Packagers transform a pair of jeans made for companies like Disney for 20 US cents each – sewed by women in Nicaragua often working 24-hour shifts, sleeping in cramped breeze-block rooms – into jeans that sell in New York or London for $20 or $30.

**Money**: No commodity can compete with money itself, which offers far bigger returns – by people who have access to almost infinite credit – than the small returns offered by any natural process. We therefore demand high returns – and are threatened with economic disaster when this inexorable growth starts to slide. When it slackens off to less than 2% a year, policy-makers become white-faced with anxiety.

**Murdoch**: then there are the taxes that benefit big over small. Poor people pay taxes when rich corporations increasingly don't. Among the big corporations that pay almost no tax worldwide is Rupert Murdoch's News Corporation. What's more, rich borrowers pay considerably less than poor borrowers (see p 93).

The result of this money insanity is all around us: identikit places, identikit culture, increasing dependence and, all over the world, bankrupt farms and suicidal farmers – like those in India who are too indebted to multinational seed companies and loan sharks to see any kind of future worth living.

*Commodity prices 1980–1997:*

| | |
|---|---|
| *Sugar* | *down 73%* |
| *Cocoa* | *down 58%* |
| *Rubber* | *down 52%* |
| *Rice* | *down 51%* |
| *Cotton* | *down 35%* |
| *Copper* | *down 30%* |

*Vandana Shiva*
*Stolen Harvest:*
*The hijacking of the global food supply*
South End Press, 1999
ISBN 0896086070

# Abstractions

## Towards a post-autistic economics

*"Where is the wisdom we have lost in knowledge?*
*Where is the knowledge we have lost in information?"*
T. S. Eliot

Hard numerical skills are valued by our society, though numbers are incapable of summing up the complexity of human truth. Meanwhile, soft human skills are down-valued. That is our tragedy and the source of so many of our basic inefficiencies and mistakes.

Of all the disciplines thus impoverished, economics has suffered the most. What began as a moral philosophy that tried to make sense of the way money behaves, has become a peculiar abstract business of formulae and statistics that bear little or no relation to the real world. Everyone knows that human beings don't actually pursue their own self-interest at all times, yet on this little lie most of economics depends. The result of this tyranny of numbers over truth is a kind of autism, according to some French economics students in 2000 who launched the Post-Autistic Economics campaign.

"It was in the beginning a modest initiative, almost confidential," wrote the French newspaper *Le Monde* in September 2000. "It has now become a subject of an important debate which has created a state of effervescence in the community of economists. Should not the teaching of economics in universities be re-thought?" A small group of students had protested on the web against the "uncontrolled use of mathematics" in economics. They claimed that mathematics had "become an end in itself", turning economics into what they called an "autistic science", dominated by abstractions that bore no relation to the real world.

Within two weeks, the petition calling for re-connection with the real world had 150 signatures, many from France's most important universities. Soon newspapers and TV stations all over France had picked up the story and even senior professors were starting a similar petition of their own. By the autumn, the campaign had led to a major debate at the Sorbonne and the French education minister, Jack Lang, had promised to set up a commission to investigate the situation and come up with some proposals to change economics teaching.

By then, there had also been a vitriolic exchange of articles by French and American economists, a counter-petition launched by MIT, and a peculiar Post-Autistic petition from Cambridge Ph.d students – unusual in that the signatories were too scared for their future careers to put their real names to it.

The Post-Autistic Economics movement has failed so far to create a widespread public debate, but they have created the first dent in the previously unassailable idea that people's individual and very human behaviour could somehow be summed up in a set of mathematical equations.

# Forgery

## The scourge of fake money

The Bank of England began issuing bank notes in 1694, printed in black. Soon, the country was over-run with counterfeits and they had to buy in special watermarked paper from Sweden. Meanwhile, the Royal Bank of Scotland had to close early in winter for fear of taking coins that had had their edges cut off by mistake in the poor afternoon light. It was they who first thought of multi-coloured banknotes printed on both sides.

> *"There wouldn't be such a thing as counterfeit gold if there were no real gold somewhere."*
> Sufi proverb

Being a banker was tough in the days when most British banks and all American banks used to print their own banknotes. With thousands of different varieties in circulation, American shops needed to keep a big tome called a Universal Counterfeit Detector by the till to distinguish the 30,000 different notes in circulation.

In the days of 'wildcat banking', anyone could set up a bank in the Wild West, print notes, pay for everything they needed – and then simply disappear. Wildcat banking wasn't all bad: it made money available to poor farmers who never would have been lent it by conventional banks. But it gave the USA two centuries of ruinous bank crashes, like the one in the film *It's a Wonderful Life*. When the US government started printing the dollar 'greenbacks' in 1862, it was all over for the wildcat banks, but not for forgery.

The biggest attempted forgery in history was a breath-taking piece of Nazi economic warfare, printing £135 million in forged pound notes in concentration camps, intending to flood the British economy. The plan was impractical so they used the forgeries instead for projects that required heavy payments – like Mussolini's rescue.

Strangely enough, old-fashioned forgery is on the increase – mainly computer-generated counterfeit money, which from $6.1 million in 1997 has been rising steadily ever since. (Every year, British bankers confiscate £80,000 in perfectly good notes that appear forged after going through the washing machine and they end up with the other six tons of old banknotes which are withdrawn every day in the UK.)

But then, what is fake? When the US dollar is backed by such a weight of debt, and by peoples' confidence that it will be repaid, that reality may be a problem there too. And these days when bank notes are replaced every few months, and coins are downright inconvenient, the worlds of reality and unreality in money are strangely overlapping. For example:

• About a quarter of a million dollars in new counterfeit money appears daily in the USA.

• Bank notes were once turned into fertiliser when they were withdrawn, but are now often made out of polymer plastic and eventually melted down and used to make plastic wheelbarrows.

• One British bank which accidentally ordered six million 50p pieces discussed putting them in landfill rather than expensively storing them.

• Parker Brothers have printed more Monopoly money than the US Federal Reserve has issued real money. A stack of all the Monopoly money they have made would be over 1,100 miles tall.

• You can buy million-dollar bills on-line that look and feel like the real thing, for 10 cents.

• $220 million in reproduction dollar bills fluttered off a film set in Las Vegas in 2003 and was spent by passers-by.

David Sinclair
*The Pound: A Biography*
Arrow, 2001
ISBN 0099406063

# Great crashes 1

## From Tulipmania to the South Seas

*"Speculators may do no harm as bubbles on a steady stream of enterprise, but the position is serious when enterprise becomes the bubble on a whirlpool of speculation."*
John Maynard Keynes, *The General Theory of Employment, Interest and Money*

The money system is supposed to work because people invest in shares issued to raise the capital that business needs to start up. That situation has now reversed itself: we raise money occasionally through shares but the vast speculative bonanza that takes place on the share markets 24 hours a day across the world is the dominant theme (see p 42).

Occasionally bonanzas cross some invisible line and become quite insane, overturning the status quo and threatening nations with anarchy. Even by the beginning of the 18th century, Jonathan

Swift (author of *Gulliver's Travels*) was risking arrest by publishing his diatribes against powerful men who pulled the strings behind the speculation.

But by then, the bizarre effects of financial 'bubbles' – when suddenly society goes crazy for dreams of untold wealth and nearly ruins itself in the process – had become clear. The 'Tulipmania' in the Netherlands in the 1630s was one of the first bubbles of the modern world. The tulip-

jobbers speculated in the rise and fall in the price of the tulip bulbs, and many grew suddenly rich when that speculation went out of control.

Writing two centuries later, Charles MacKay, author of *Extraordinary Popular Delusions and the Madness of Crowds* described how "nobles, citizens, farmers, mechanics, seamen, footmen, maid-servants, even chimney-sweeps and old clotheswomen, dabbled in tulips. People of all grades converted their property into cash, and invested it in flowers. Houses and lands were offered for sale at ruinously low prices, or assigned in payment of bargains made at the tulip-mart. Foreigners became smitten with the same frenzy, and money poured into Holland from all directions. The prices of the necessities of life rose again by degrees: houses and lands, horses and carriages, and luxuries of every sort rose in value with them, and Holland seemed the very anti-chamber of Plutus."

Tulip bulbs that had been bought for people's gardens suddenly reached extraordinary prices, and the rarest were bought for speculation. Strange stories circulated about people who bought them thinking they were onions, ate them by mistake, and found they had consumed the value of a large mansion.

Then the bottom dropped out of the market, the speculators were ruined and aristocrats had to mortgage their estates. Everyone vowed it would never happen again. It always does – with the same patterns: a belief that some new technological or economic breakthrough has permanently changed the way markets react; doubters are publicly ridiculed, funds for useful projects dry up, and there are assurances that this time it will be different.

Scottish financier John Law persuaded the French government to set up the Banque Royale in 1717, through which he issued large numbers of bank notes which were to be underpinned by profits from his speculative Mississippi Company. There were riots at the Bourse in Paris as people fought, and even sold their bodies, for the right to buy shares. The company was soon so successful that Law agreed to take on the entire French national debt, turned it into paper and became the richest man in the world.

Fearful that his monster would run out of steam, he employed navvies to march through Paris – ostensibly on their way to South America to dig for gold. But it didn't work. In 1720 the bubble burst and Law escaped with his life to die in poverty in Venice. The French aristocracy and middle classes were ruined. The ground had been laid for the revolution.

At the same time the London-based South Sea Company was taking over the British national debt, and speculation in its shares multiplied their value ten times over. Copycat companies joined in the fray with bizarre schemes to develop perpetual motion machines, to trade in hair, to insure horses, or "for carrying on an undertaking of great advantage, which shall be revealed later".

When the chairman and some of the directors of the South Sea Company sold out, the bubble began to deflate, with similar disastrous effects on anyone who had gone from rags to riches as a result. One of the few to sell in time was a small bookseller called Thomas Guy: he was so thankful to escape with his new wealth that he founded Guy's Hospital in London.

In the following century, there was the disastrous speculation in railway shares in the 1840s. Then again, 50 years later, the Bank of England had to save Barings Bank from collapse after speculation in Argentinian shares. And so on.

Each bubble is followed by an orgy of blame and regulation, which never seems to prevent a recurrence, because of one key omission. "Nobody blamed the credulity and avarice of the people – the degrading lust of gain," said Charles MacKay, writing about the South Sea Bubble at the time of the Railway Bubble. "Or the infatuation which had made the multitude run their heads with such frantic eagerness into the net held out for them by scheming projectors. These things were never mentioned."

They never are.

*Edward Chancellor*
*Devil Take the Hindmost:*
*A history of financial speculation*
Macmillan, 2000
ISBN 330484095

# Great crashes 2

## Wall Street 1929

*"No Congress of the United States ever assembled, on surveying the state of the Union, has met with a more pleasing prospect than that which appears at the present time."*
President Calvin Coolidge in 1928. The crash happened less than a year later.

Nearly every generation believes its own situation is uniquely safe. Take, for example, the designers of the *Titanic* in 1912 or the designers of the US Federal Reserve system the following year. By the 1920s it was widely believed that the 'Fed' provided the perfect financial safety net, controlling interest rates and money supply by buying and selling government bonds.

It was the era of Henry Ford's production lines and Frederick Taylor's fearsome stop-watch. The combination of modern factories and new theories on time and motion was believed to

have created a new 'science' of management. This was a time of rising productivity, docile trade unions, new technologies like radio storming up the stock market, not to mention tax and interest rate cuts; the market seemed unstoppable. No wonder that the world's leading economist, Prof Irving Fisher, believed by 1928 that "stock prices have reached what looks like a permanently high plateau".

An enormous new industry selling stocks was competing to push new ones even faster onto the market. Around 600 new brokerage houses opened on Wall Street in 1928 and 1929. A new investment house opened its doors every day for the first nine months of 1929, issuing $2.5 billion in securities to the public – half of which would shortly turn out to be worthless. "No-one can examine the panorama of business and finance in America during the past half-dozen years without realising that we are living in a new era," said John Moody, founder of the credit ratings agency.

Everyone wanted bit. There were special rooms in hotels on Broadway for wealthy women to play the market, much to the disapproval of the more traditional brokers. "Everybody ought to be rich," said the title of a long essay by John Raskob of General Motors in the *Ladies Home Journal* of August 1929, explaining that $10,000 invested in General Motors a decade before was now worth $1.5 million.

You couldn't lose. There wasn't even any need for a financial adviser, said Groucho Marx, who borrowed a quarter of a million dollars to play the market: "You could close your eyes, stick your finger on the big board and the stock you bought would start rising."

This was dangerous. People borrowed to invest, believing that the market would just keep rising. 'Margin loans' used shares from previous investments as security for the new borrowings; this was to cause a devastating unravelling when the market turned.

The market reached its height in early September 1929, and from October a series of terrifying lurches wiped 83% off the value of American investments. With every lurch, the shares underwriting people's loans lost value too, forcing inexorable rounds of selling and heart-breaking overnight bankruptcies. Groucho Marx, Irving Berlin and Winston Churchill were among those who lost a fortune – so was Irving Fisher.

"We have involved ourselves in a colossal muddle," said Keynes a few years later, "having blundered in the control of a delicate machine, the working of which we do not understand."

In 1933, the US Congress passed the Glass-Steagall Act to place a strict wall between commercial and investment banking so that a crash never happened again. They busily repealed it again during the dot.com boom of the 1990s. We still don't understand the critical importance of the right kind of regulations.

John Kenneth Galbraith
*The Great Crash 1929*
Penguin Books, 1988
ISBN 0140136096

# Great crashes 3

## Junk bonds

*"The point is, ladies and gentleman, that greed, for lack of a better word, is good. Greed is right. Greed works."*
Gordon Gekko, *Wall Street*, 1987

The explosion of greed in New York, Tokyo and London in the 1980s was partly the result of the deregulation policies of Margaret Thatcher and Ronald Reagan, but – as the party got up steam – it was junk bonds that turned it into a full-scale furnace.

Bonds are simply agreements to pay a specific sum on a specific date in return for a loan. Junk bonds are those that are rated riskier than investment grade; the risk is that the issuer won't pay. The upside is that junk bonds have a higher yield and they allowed companies that couldn't get conventional backing to launch themselves, including the contemporary giants MCI, Viacom and Turner Broadcasting. The downside is that some of them were extremely risky.

"The securities involve a high degree of risk," said the front page of one junk bond prospectus two days after the 1987 Crash, "and accordingly, investors may lose their entire investment."

But that didn't matter. The first new junk bond was issued in 1977 and soon a third of all new bond issues were junk. The revolution came courtesy of the 'Junk Bond King', Michael Milken of Drexel Burnham in Los Angeles, whose new idea launched a wave of hostile takeovers of well-known companies like TWA and RJR Nabisco – dramatised in one of the most successful business books of all time, *Barbarians at the Gate*.

These were known as Leveraged Buy-Outs (LBOs). What the corporate raiders did was to issue junk bonds in the name of the company they were trying to take over, using any available credit the target company had to take them over. Companies that had carefully stayed out of debt became prime targets. Once they had taken them over and sold off the profitable parts, rigorous restructuring was necessary to pay the interest on the great burdens of debt. Tens of thousands of workers lost jobs.

Milken's Drexel Burnham High Yield Bond Conference became known as the 'Predators' Ball' because the most important guests were the corporate raiders who used his junk bonds.

Milken got extremely rich, earning a reported $550 million in 1987 alone, but by then the federal prosecutors were investigating. The 1987 Crash also wiped about a quarter of the value of companies on Wall Street overnight. He and others were indicted by a federal grand jury in 1989 on 98 counts of racketeering and fraud. A year later, he was sentenced to 10 years in prison. He served two years and is now banned for life from financial services, and spends his time managing a network of charities and think-tanks.

> *Junk Bond wisdom:*
> *"Greed is alright, by the way. You can be greedy and still feel good about yourself."*
> Ivan Boesky, who made an 80% gain on his investments in the 1980s and ended up in jail.

James Grant
*The Trouble with Prosperity*
John Wiley, 1998
ISBN 0471984795

# Great crashes 4

## The dot.com explosion

*"Never before have so many unskilled 24-year-olds made so much money in so little time as we did this decade in New York and London."*
Michael Lewis in *Liar's Poker*

The tech stocks phenomenon of the late 1990s had all the characteristics of a classic bubble: a technological development was supposed completely to remake the economy, nothing would ever be the same again, and the doubters were ridiculed in the press. For a moment, they had many people believing that a web site like @Home was suddenly worth the same as Lockheed Martin, or the internet share-trader E*Trade was worth the same as the giant American Airlines.

Tiny AOL even took over the giant media empire Time Warner – one of the most disastrous mergers of all time. Most of the dot.coms have now disappeared, and even E*Trade decided to open its own bricks and mortar banks.

A handful survived the crash – Amazon, eBay, Lastminute.com and a few others – but the rest were swept away. The whole idea of investors falling over themselves to hand cash to pushy 20-somethings, with business plans that had no obvious way of making any money back, lasted only a few years.

But once again, those caught up in the bubble believed that this time everything would be different. "We have one general response to the word 'valuation' these days: 'Bull market'," said Morgan Stanley's Mary Meeker, the so-called Queen of the Net. "We believe we have entered a new valuation zone."

Meeker was paid $15 million by Morgan Stanley in her top year, 1999, for giving advice to investors. The trouble is that the Chinese walls that should separate investor advice from the other banking operations in Wall Street had disappeared. Other tech stock analysts were now supposed to look out for promising companies, sit in on strategy sessions, take new companies public, and – by implication – provide favourable advice that helped sell their shares. Most Wall Street analysts' pay was linked to the banking deals they were involved with. 'Advice' was no longer 'detached'.

Meanwhile, the anonymous web bulletin boards hyped pointless dot.com projects and fed the frenzy. By the time sanity emerged, the IT industry suffered the equivalent of the South Sea Bubble scandal many times over.

Behind the dot.com scandal was the even more peculiar story of the unfolding telecommunications disaster. Thrilled by the prospect of data traffic doubling every three or four months indefinitely, telecom firms around the world put down fibre-optic cable as fast as they could. The work has cost some $4,000 billion over the past five years,

at least half of it borrowed (the entire output of the US economy is about $10,000 billion). The interest on these staggering loans, and the vast sums paid in the UK for third-generation cellphone licenses, crippled the telecoms giants, and they were forced to sack half a million people worldwide

Dot.coms, telecoms and the strange world of accounting that hyped the profits of companies like Enron – which claimed to be a dot.com – all made the turn of the century one of the oddest periods on Wall Street.

> *Fines paid by J P Morgan Chase and Citigroup for their role in the Enron fraud - $286m*
> *Fees they received from Enron in previous five years - $300m*

John Cassidy
*Dot.con: The real story of why the internet bubble burst*
Penguin, 2002
ISBN 0141006668

# Great crashes 5

## Derivatives

Welcome to the modern world of arcane financial instruments, and perhaps even to the world of the next Great Crash. Derivatives are fiendishly complex, and they cover anything that isn't tangible: the right to buy raw materials at a future date at a set price, or the underwriting of a risk that someone won't be paid by someone else. Derivatives are not about the rate of growth but the rate that growth is growing, and the rate that 'second' growth is growing too.

*"Derivatives are financial instruments of mass destruction."*
Warren Buffett, the world's most successful investor, Fortune, 17 March 2003

It's all about offsetting risk – because it's all about buying options on shares rather than the shares themselves – and that can be useful for companies. But derivatives deals that go wrong can multiply losses many times over, and that can be disastrous too.

The first hint of trouble in the early 1990s hit the German company Metallgesellschaft, followed in quick succession by nine-figure losses by Cargill, Procter & Gamble, Daiwa Bank of Japan and Orange County, California – before Nick Leeson's bet on a rising Japanese stock market in 1995 destroyed the 225-year-old Barings Bank.

Then there was Long Term Capital Management (LTCM), run by brilliant market people. The idea was to hedge and protect their bets, using $3 billion they had been lent to buy derivatives with a notional value of $1,250 billion. But the Russian debt crisis of 1998 upset their complex mathematical predictions and they were soon losing $500 million a day. The US Federal Reserve was afraid for the world's banking system and bailed them out with $3.6 billion.

Even so, by 2001, an astonishing $44,000 billion was invested in derivatives in Wall Street alone, more than half of that in the powerful bank JPMorganChase – including so many options on gold that they controlled the entire world's output for two and a half years ahead.

Even the Bank of England was warning about the threat to global financial stability. To put JPMorganChase's derivatives into perspective: the entire losses on the world's stock markets between 2000-3 were only $7,000 billion. No wonder the bank was nervous.

But the risk is vague because the experts on derivatives hide away in the secretive hedge funds – using derivatives to make money as markets slide. They reveal nothing, not even who works for them. Hedge funds tend to be registered in offshore financial centres (see p 52), and market themselves just to the very rich. Managers tend to take 1% of the invested funds and 20% of the profits in their pay packet, so the results have to be spectacular. These days the most famous hedge fund managers, George Soros, Julian Robertson and Barton Biggs, are shifting to a new generation of even more shadowy and unregulated successors.

Some of them are also immensely ambitious. Soros made $2 billion when he led the run on the pound on Black Wednesday in 1992, when it dropped out of the European Monetary System. It also seems likely that there was a tacit conspiracy among hedge funds, during the financial crisis of 1998, to target the Australian dollar. In fact some hedge fund managers warned the Australian treasury that resistance was futile.

But was the conspiracy bigger than that? Some economists believe the whole crisis of 1997/8 – with hospital patients across the Far East thrown out of their beds and onto the street because their currencies had collapsed – was the result of a hedge fund conspiracy that went out of control.

Derivatives need serious regulation, before it's too late.

Peter Temple
*Hedge Funds:*
*The courtesans of capital*
John Wiley, 2001
ISBN 0471899739

# Calming the money flows

## The Tobin Tax

*"The collapse of the global marketplace would be a traumatic event with unimaginable consequences. Yet I find it easier to imagine than the continuation of the present regime."*
George Soros, *Soros on Soros*

The financial establishment believes that the sloshing of vast sums of money across the wires of the money system – $2,000 billion a day, remember, most of it speculation – makes the economic system efficient. The traders react quickly to efficient governments by buying their currency – and just as quickly by punishing inefficient ones.

George Soros and his Quantum Fund were, between them, the most famous hedge fund double act in the world during the 1990s – until he withdrew from active management after mis-timing his reaction to the dot.com boom and

losing a packet. It was Soros who was one of the first insiders to warn the world of the perils of the system's built-in instability: traders earn more when the market veers wildly than they do when it is stable.

It isn't just the dangerous interconnections in the global marketplace (see p 42), or the computers that are programmed to sell automatically when the market drops a certain amount.

The whole theory is flawed, said Soros: it doesn't tend towards equilibrium at all, but overshoots and veers dangerously off in the wrong direction.

In the 1998 crisis, where currency after currency across the Far East collapsed in the markets – with devastating consequences for the people who lived there – people began to ask whether there were alternatives. Or at least some speed bumps to slow down the flow of capital. Even Tony Blair began talking about the consequences of an "absence of discipline" in the markets.

Here are some possible solutions:

The Malaysia solution: Malaysian prime minister Mohamed Mahathir re-established exchange controls, preventing people taking large sums of money out of the country – the situation all over the world until 1979. The Malaysian recovery was faster than their neighbours'.

The Columbia solution: letting foreigners invest in local businesses but not to buy debt or shares, which means they can't simply sell-up over night..

The Chile solution: any foreigners investing in the country have to keep their money there for a year – which deters speculators.

The Tobin solution: this was the brainwave of the Nobel prize-winning economist James Tobin, who suggested a small levy on foreign exchange transactions of 0.05 per cent. This would be enough to calm down the speculation, but it would also raise enough money to put the UN sustainable development programme into effect.

The Tobin Levy is very controversial – Tobin himself changed his mind about it – but has been backed at various times by the Canadian and the French governments. It would fail if one of the main financial centres remained aloof, and they would all have to agree. But if governments were allowed to keep half the money they collect from it, that might be a sufficient reward to get them moving.

> *Proportion of world economic activity which is foreign speculation - 97%*
>
> *Proportion in the 1970s - 30%*
>
> *Proportion of countries to face a major currency or banking crisis since 1990 - 25%*

# The new multi-billionnaires

## The world of Bill Gates

*"Money is like muck, not good except it be spread."*
Francis Bacon

One peculiarity of the speculative 'success' of recent years is how little has trickled down. The economist Paul Krugman estimates that up to 70% of the extraordinary US economic growth of the 1980s was delivered to the richest 1% of the population. There were 13 billionnaires in the USA in 1982, and by 1999 there were 268 – and that was before the dot.com boom.

Similar disparities exist between the people of the world as a whole. The poorest 20% of countries now have less than 1% of world trade (a quarter of what it was a generation ago).

The vast wealth has been partly driven by ridiculous pay-packages for chief executives, often no matter how unsuccessful they are. Disney's CEO Michael Eisner was paid a package worth $575 million in 1998 – about 25,070 times the average Disney worker's pay (and far more than that if you count the low wages paid in factories in Honduras or Bangladesh that make Disney shirts and bags).

Of all the wealthy individuals, the most outrageously so has been Microsoft founder Bill Gates. When Windows 2000 was launched, Gates' personal stock of Microsoft shares rose in value by more than $130 billion – or 12 times more than the entire securities owned by the whole population of African-Americans.

Yet super-managers were also being rewarded for driving down the wages of those at the bottom end – increasingly seeking out immigrants who are ignorant of their rights, which is why, even in the USA, the average wage has been sinking slowly since the 1960s.

The question is whether democracy can survive with gigantic disparities in wealth and power, or whether, as the economist Jeff Gates puts it, the system is "making the world safe for plutocracy". For example:

• Three billion of the world's population live on less than $2 a day.

• The world's 200 biggest corporations account for 28% of world economic activity but employ less than 0.25% of the global workforce.

• The world's 200 wealthiest people – who doubled their net worth between 1994-9 – own the same amount of wealth as the combined annual income of the poorest 2.5 billion people.

• African-Americans owned 0.5% of the net worth of the USA in 1865, the year slavery was abolished. By 1990 this had crawled up to 1%.

• A fighter aircraft sold to a poor country costs the same as education for three million children in the Third World.

Does anyone in the world really deserve to be paid more than £1 million? Executives are now credited with extra years to their pensions as a way of getting round criticisms about pay – often while they are busily cutting the pension rights of employees (see p 97). The US Treasury Secretary, John Snow, was credited with 19 extra years that he hadn't worked by his previous employer CSX, which he then took as a lump sum worth $33 million.

## Wall Street pay packets

| | Pay in 2002 | Change in co. value in 2002 |
|---|---|---|
| Steve Jobs | | |
| *Apple* | $78m | down 35% |
| David Cote | | |
| *Honeywell* | $68m | down 27% |
| John Chambers | | |
| *Cisco* | $55m | down 28% |
| Pat Russo | | |
| *Lucent* | $38m | down 75% |

Jeff Gates
*Democracy at Risk: Rescuing Main Street from Wall Street*
Perseus, 2001
ISBN 0738204838
Bottom of Form

Section VI

# DIY money

What do neighbourhoods and towns do when they are sidelined by the global money superhighway? Well, for a start, they can try creating their own…

# Creating money

## The challenge of doing it yourself

*"Singapore and Hong Kong, which are oddities today, have their own currencies and so they possess this built-in advantage. They have no need of tariffs or export subsidies. Their currencies serve those functions when needed, but only as long as needed. Detroit, on the other hand, has no such advantage. When its export work first began to decline it got no feedback, so Detroit merely declined, uncorrected."*
Jane Jacobs, *Cities and the Wealth of Nations*, discussing the advantages of city currencies.

Banks create money, governments create cash, businesses create shares – so why can't we all create the money we need?

This isn't something we can do entirely by ourselves – though David Bowie was one individual who managed to issue Bowie Bonds as a way of drawing forward some of his future income. But when

communities, neighbourhoods, towns or cities run short of cash – because it has all flowed somewhere more lucrative – then it can make sense to issue their own.

National currencies tend to be geared to the financial services sector – just as the pound and the dollar are. They are information systems that respond to the values that Wall Street and the City

of London feel are important, but they don't circulate nearly so well – for example – in manufacturing areas or in poorer suburbs.

Yet those marginalised places may have everything they need for success: people who want to work, people who need jobs done, raw materials that can be put to use – but not have the cash they need to bring them all together. The banks won't create it for them, and the investment money may prefer to shoot down the wires to the City to frolic among the hedge funds or dot.coms or whatever clever scheme is in vogue at the time. Creating their own may be the imaginative leap they need.

Creating your own cash has a long and honourable tradition. It wasn't until the 12th or 13th century that kings tried to get control of all the money – and a terrible hash of it they have made ever since. In the USA it wasn't until the end of the Civil War that the US government took the exclusive power to issue cash themselves – though of course banks can do the same using a signature on a cheque or a computer keystroke. Since then, the following

has been used as money when the 'real' stuff got scarce:

Beads and precious stones: the early settlers in North America bought Manhattan island from the native Americans for $24 worth of beads.

Tea: the Chinese used square packs of tea. The original Chinese word for these was 'cash'.

Tobacco, especially in wartime, when cigarettes used to become universal currency – especially the bad ones. (The good ones got smoked.)

Paper: Benjamin Franklin's efforts at the printing press were one of the many causes of the American War of Independence (see p 36).

Air miles: Northwest Airlines paid their entire public relations budget in air miles throughout the 1990s.

Tokens: the Global Barter Clubs of Argentina now have over a million members, using tokens as currency, allowing people to barter surplus stock, vegetables and other mutual support.

Out-of-date stock: up to a fifth of world trade is now carried out using electronic barter currencies like trade dollars (see p 162).

If they can do it, why should impoverished towns and communities wait helplessly around for the government to rescue them – when they know perfectly well they won't – and when they have all the bare necessities they need locally. They can issue their own money and start using their own assets more efficiently.

That's what different kinds of money do: they are information systems that measure the value of local assets differently from the big currencies. Big currencies don't see local young people, old people, dilapidated buildings, or parks as assets. They don't realise that all the computers, white goods and furniture we throw away in perfect working order are actually assets. If we can design currencies that value them better, then they will be used.

That's the challenge for the DIY currency experts, and it's one they meet in a variety of ways. They know their new currencies need to be backed by something – whether this be the trust of the people who use them, local produce (see p 146), locally-produced renewable energy or other commodities – otherwise nobody will use them. They also know they need to be available enough to be useful, otherwise only the rich will get them. Every DIY currency mixes these functions – free money (medium of exchange) and real money (store of value) in different ways. That's the point about money: it has to be real but it also has to be available.

Yet most modern money achieves neither of these. It is 'fiat' money, created out of nothing by banks and worth something because the governments say it is. ('Fiat' comes from 'fiat lux' from the first verse of Genesis: 'let there be light'.) We need new kinds of money, invested in new ways, to put local people and small business first. You won't get rich inventing your own money – though some of the dot.com internet currencies like beenz and i-points did briefly turn their creators into multi-millionaires on paper. But it could get the exhausted wheels of the local economy turning again, and it could provide new values to the money system that it now conspicuously lacks.

Thomas Greco
*Money: Understanding and creating alternatives to legal tender*
Chelsea Green, 2000
ISBN 1890132373

# Money that rusts

## Irving Fisher and stamp scrip

*"The purpose of Free-Money is to break the unfair privilege enjoyed by money. This unfair privilege is solely due to the fact that the traditional form of money has one immense advantage over all other goods, namely that it is indestructible."*
Silvio Gesell, the Argentinian trader who came up with the idea of rusting money.

It is always going to be easier to make money out of money, rather than using it to do something productive, said the Argentinian trader Silvio Gesell in 1913. Because money grows if you invest it – but real commodities tend to rust or go mouldy.

The answer, he said, is to have money that rusts too. The idea was taken up enthusiastically during the Great Depression, most dramatically in the Austrian skiing town of Wörgl. And by catching the eye of the great American

economist Irving Fisher, rusting money was adopted all over the world before it was declared illegal by the world's central banks, fearful of a threat to their own authority.

As a result, only one of the great 1930s money experiments is still running: the Wir system in Switzerland, a mutual-credit currency scheme widely used by the building industry and the restaurant sector. Wir started in 1934, the brainchild of Werner Zimmerman and Paul Enz, two followers of Gesell. By 1993, it had a turnover of £12 billion and 65,000 corporate members, using a parallel currency to the Swiss franc.

Wörgl was in a terrible state in the Great Depression when the burgomaster Michael

Unterguggenberger persuaded the town to issue its own currency, to the value of 30,000 Austrian schillings, known as 'tickets for services rendered'. But unlike ordinary money, these notes lost value by 1% a month, and to keep value – if you hadn't spent – you had to buy their stamps once a month and stick them on the back. The proceeds of the stamps went on poor relief.

The notes circulated incredibly fast. Within 24 hours of being issued, most of them had not only come back, via shops and businesses, to the municipality in the form of tax payments – sometimes months in advance – but had already been passed on their way again. During the first month, the money made the complete circle no fewer than 20 times. After four months, the town had built public works of 100,000 schillings, employing people who were jobless; most of the town's tax arrears had been paid off too.

Fisher was inspired by what he found in Austria and rushed out his own instruction manuals, called 'Stamp Scrip', for the struggling American towns. Within months, about 300 US communities were printing their own negative-interest money.

Then, on 4 March 1933, it was all over. President Roosevelt, advised that the monetary system was in danger, banned scrip systems and gave the existing ones a short time to wind themselves up.

As he did so, he also created the conditions for a final flurry of activity. Fearing a complete collapse of the American banking system, he closed all the banks – and all over the country, communities and companies had to provide some kind of alternative to money. "I care not what kind – silver, copper, brass, gold or paper," said one senator from Oklahoma. One community in Tenino in Washington state even produced its own wooden money.

But Roosevelt, who famously declared on that day in March that "we have nothing to fear but fear itself", needed to allay the fears of his 'sound money' bankers and economists. As a result, local money disappeared for two or three generations. Still, it was the velocity of the money that appealed to Fisher. If the American government couldn't persuade banks to risk lending people's savings, then you could set up local money which kept circulating and didn't disappear into the banks of the wealthiest. Stamp scrip was like blood. As the stamp scrips were shut down on one side of the Atlantic, the Austrian National Bank was taking action to suppress the Worgl experiment too. Four years later, Austria was annexed by Nazi Germany.

These days, the fiddly business of sticking on stamps is unnecessary, because computers can do those calculations. Stamp scrip might not provide the stability people need for real money – money they can use for savings – but it might as well serve for exchange money. We can still learn something from Gesell, Fisher and Unterguggenberger.

Richard Douthwaite
*Short Circuit: Strengthening local economies for security in an unstable world*
Green Books, 1996
ISBN 1870098641

# Real money

## Keeping it constant

*"For in every country of the world, I believe, the avarice and injustice of princes and sovereign states abusing the confidence of their subjects, have by degrees diminished the real quality of the metal, which had been originally contained in their coins."*
Adam Smith

People become interested in creating their own money in times of economic hardship. When that hardship is a clampdown on the amount of money in the economy, then people look for ways of creating currencies that are more available. But when the hardship is spiralling inflation, they look for something that is more reliable.

One of the most fascinating experiments in creating money in the 1970s was for an inflation-busting currency and it was the brainchild of Ralph Borsodi – then in his 80s, and one of the founders of the green movement. He warned of inflation a good quarter century before it became a problem (the only bestseller he ever wrote was called *Inflation is Coming*), and he predicted the post-war flight from the cities on both sides of the Atlantic. He also worked with Irving Fisher during the Depression to help him develop his 'Stamp Scrip' (see 141).

By the 1970s, enraged by growing inflation around the world, which he regarded as a government fraud on the public, he became fascinated with the possibility of inventing a new kind of money that would keep its value because it was based on something real. Over lunch in Escondido, California in 1972, he picked up a copy of the *New York Times* and found that the Federal Reserve was devaluing the dollar. In a rage, he sat down and designed what he called an 'honest money system'.

Later that year he launched the 'constant' currency in his home town of Exeter, New Hampshire. What was revolutionary about the 'constant' was that its value was tied to a basket of commodities. It was also backed by $100,000 of his own money, on deposit in banks in Exeter, Boston and London.

Borsodi's main problems were: how to choose these commodities, how to buy them as backing, and how to store them. You couldn't put $100,000 worth of oil and wheat in your garage, let alone in the bank. So he arbitraged them instead, organising a team of supporters to buy shiploads of the chosen commodities while they were at sea in tankers and sell them straight on – and meanwhile make a profit.

By February 1973, the University of New Hampshire Press was printing 275,000 'constants' in different denominations up to 100. Exeter's local council even started accepting them as payment for parking fines. His economist friends at the university were working out how to keep the value steady, while young volunteers dealt with paperwork and the media. Bemused locals tried to understand why their constants were worth $2 one week, but only $2.05 a week or so later.

Having proved that a constant value was possible and that people would use it, Borsodi wound the experiment up. It has never been repeated. His main disappointment was that it failed to enrage the Federal Reserve. But officials were relaxed about it: "They can circulate clamshells or pine cones if they want to," they told the press. "As long as people accept them." Attitudes have changed. Three decades on, starting your own currency remains legal – through there are now regulations governing e-currencies.

David Boyle
*Funny Money:*
*In search of alternative cash*
HarperCollins/Flamingo, 1999
ISBN 0002559471

# Money as vegetables

## Printing your own

*"I guess the only solution is to print your own money."*
Frank Tortoriello, Deli Diner, Great Barrington, Massachusetts

Frank Tortoriello was the proprietor of a small deli diner in the Massachusetts town of Great Barrington, when he was turned down by his bank for a $5,000 bank loan to move to bigger premises. When he asked the E. F. Schumacher Society, based nearby, for advice they suggested that he issue his own money.

The result was deli dollars, a series of notes designed by a local artist and marked "redeemable for meals up to a value of ten dollars". The Deli would not be able to redeem all the notes at once after the move, so Frank staggered repayment over a year by placing a 'valid after' date on each note. To discourage counterfeiting, he signed every note individually like a cheque, and he sold them for $8 each. He raised $5,000 in a month.

The notes were an enormous success. Contractors bought sets of deli dollars as Christmas presents for their construction crews, parents of students at the nearby college knew they would make a good gift for their children. Even the bankers who turned down the original loan request supported Frank by buying them. The notes turned up in the collection plate of the First Congregational Church because church-goers knew the minister ate breakfast at the Deli. Frank repaid the loan, not in dollars but in cheese-on-rye sandwiches. The idea was the brainchild of the great social innovator Bob Swann, a carpenter who spent two years in prison as a conscientious objector during World War II, much of it in solitary confinement because he refused to accept the prison's racial segregation rules. During that time, he came under the influence of an associate of Gandhi's and found himself thinking deeply about money. Under his influence, the deli dollar idea spread.

Two local farms took up the idea of issuing 'greensbacks' to recover from a fire and to help them meet the high cost of heating their greenhouses through the winter. Customers would buy the notes in the autumn for redemption in plants and vegetables in the spring and summer. The result was the Farm Preserve Note. They were designed with a head of cabbage in the middle surrounded by a variety of other vegetables. The notes read "In Farms We Trust" and were sold for $9 each.

The farm preserve notes, Monterey general store notes, and Kintaro notes that followed gave local residents a way to vote for the kind of small independent businesses that help to make a local economy more self-reliant.

Swann was concerned about underpinning the value of the money – but also of making it more available by basing its value on local products that are universally available, like locally-produced energy, or chickens, or firewood. The point is, we have these assets locally, and they can be used to raise money. We are not as poor or dependent as we think.

# DIY money 1

## LETS

*'On the morning after the Depression a
man came to work building a house, and
the foreman said to him, "Sorry chum you
can't work today. There ain't no inches." He
said "What do you mean there ain't no
inches? We got lumber, we got metal, we
even got tape measures." The foreman said,
"The trouble with you is you don't
understand business. There are no inches.
We have been using too many of them and
there are not enough to go around."'*
Alan Watts, *Of Time and Eternity*

One of the paradoxes of money is that it is
increasingly just blips of information (see p 50) –
just a measuring system that we pretend is also
valuable. But it does lead to some peculiarities. To
say there isn't enough money is like saying there
isn't enough inches, said the originator of LETS,
Michael Linton, making use of an example by the
philosopher Alan Watts.

And if you think about it, it is crazy. You may have
someone to do the job, the raw material for the
job and the demand for it, but no money to bring
all those things together. In 1848, the radical
Pierre-Joseph Proudhon launched a People's
Bank which – although it was swept away by that

year of revolutions – allowed the money to be created automatically by that kind of situation. The buyer would simply create a debt themselves, denominate it – not in pounds or euros – but in some agreed currency, and pay it off later by doing work themselves.

That was the idea behind the explosion in local currencies in the 1980s, starting with ideas like David Weston's Community Exchange in Vancouver and Michael Linton's Local Exchange and Trading System in Canada's Comox Valley. The idea is not just to increase the medium of exchange, but also to improve the quality rather than just the quantity of the economy.

Weston was a social innovator and academic; Linton was an Alexander Technique teacher. LETS rapidly spread across the English-speaking world in the 1980s and the French-speaking world in the 1990s, but it began as a mutual-credit money system, called 'green dollars'. People and businesses decide the rate and conditions for accepting the community currency instead of normal cash, which they can negotiate with customers. You may need cash for the tax and the cost of materials from outside the local economy, but you can use other kinds of money for other aspects of the purchase. So you issue your own money in green dollars, and by doing so, you are 'committed' to honour it, redeem your money, and keep your promise.

The transactions are tracked, normally using a computer programme. In the UK, where LETS spread to almost 400 schemes during the 1990s, a series of bizarre and colourful names were used for these – 'bricks' in Brixton or 'bobbins' in Manchester – much to the disapproval of the originators of the idea in Canada.

Linton's first LETS began in 1983: within two years, it had turned over the equivalent of $300,000 in 'green dollars' trading, including vegetables, room rents and dentistry. What is exciting about LETS is its simplicity. It did not attract the attention of regulators and officials who might have been concerned that this be some kind of 'bank'. There was also no problem about how much should be issued. The debits and credits on the system always exactly equalled each other: when you buy with LETS, you create a credit that can be spent by somebody else. LETS is normally taxable, like barter trade dollars, but governments have generally been confused about how to treat LETS for welfare purposes. New Zealand and the Netherlands are among those to have passed laws encouraging unemployed people to use their local currencies. UK cities like Liverpool and Sheffield have been among those experimenting with LETS as a way of building a sense of community on poverty-stricken housing estates.

The trouble with modern money is that it is issued by 'them' – banks, regulated by central banks – rather than us. Local currencies means that communities or towns or regions can issue their own, according to what they need – money that isn't loaded with complex information that makes it travel the world looking for higher returns, but which stays circulating locally.

"We have the materials, the tools, the space, the time, the skills and the intent to build – but we have no inches today" Linton wrote in his *Open Money Manifesto* (www.openmoney.org). "Why be short of inches? Why be short of money?"

Jonathan Croall
*LETS Act Locally: The growth of local exchange trading systems*
Calouste Gulbenkian Foundation, 1997
ISBN 0903319810

# DIY money 2

## Community way

Imagine a world where everyone had, not only an e-mail address, but also a cc (community currency address), and could use it to create money in as many different currencies as they might want – a village currency, a babysitting currency, a city or regional currency, or an international currency for plumbers, for example. They could suit different aspects of their lives.

The system already exists on the internet and it is breathtakingly simple, set up by the man who began LETS, Michael Linton, who has spent the last two decades working out how to make a money system that can simply provide people with what they need without having to get a bank loan.

> *"Any community, network, business, can create its own free money – 'free' as in free speech, free radical, freely available, but not free as in 'free lunch.'"*
> Michael Linton and Ernie Yacub,
> *Open Money Manifesto*

Embedded within it is a whole new idea about how communities can provide themselves with the money they need; it is sponsored by business – but costs them nothing.

This is known as 'community way', and is operating in communities on the Canadian west coast. The idea goes like this:

• Local businesses create the electronic local money in the form of donations to local charities (at no cash cost to them because this is local money, though they do have to pay for the electronic equipment).

• Next the charities sell these electronic points to local donors in return for pounds or dollars.

• They then use the local money to buy what they want – all the participating businesses agree to accept it on their own terms, maybe 20, 50 or even 80 per cent of the normal price – whatever ensures that their basic cash costs (including taxes) are covered in national money.

• It carries on circulating until it returns to the original business that issued it, which is then encouraged to spend or donate it on again, keeping the loop going.

It sounds like a trick, but it isn't. Businesses accept local money to attract new customers, and it saves them money off their marketing budget. Everybody wins, because local businesses are playing the same role as banks – creating money out of nothing. And the local money keeps the lifeblood of the local community working.

There are plans to try the idea in a big city, using smartcards, as well as the phone, internet and paper registers, which make the necessary dual-currency transactions a bit smoother.

'Community way' is an imaginative response to the way some local communities are running out of cash, and it is has already worked.

**In rural Ireland**: the 'roma' currency (Roscommon Mayo) was run as an EU-funded experiment. Roma notes were issued into the local economy by the local radio station. They then circulated and were eventually accepted back in return for advertising.

**In Minneapolis**: the Commonweal project developed a dual-track credit card, with dollars and time credits earned helping out in the community. They were accepted as part payment for goods and services in the biggest shopping mall in the USA, outside Minneapolis.

The point of Commonweal, said inventor Joel Hodroff, was that the mainstream economy was infinitely productive. That meant you could take points like babysitting credits and give them buying power in the main economy. Restaurants that struggled to cover costs on Sundays could attract new diners by accepting part payment in credits, while covering their costs in dollars.

Taken together, these ideas and community way provide the basis for a whole new multi-currency world – using different credit systems to underpin different aspects of our lives.

# DIY money 3

## Hours

*"Hours is money with a boundary around it, so it stays in our community. It doesn't come to town, shake a few hands and then wander out across the globe. It reinforces trading locally."*
Paul Glover, founder of Ithaca hours

The kind of DIY money you design depends on what specific problem you are trying to solve. And one of the key problems with modern money for towns like Ithaca in upstate New York is that money won't just stay put.

A generation ago money earned in a community would stay there circulating like lifeblood (see p 47), and every time it was spent in the small shops it would carry on going round, bringing wealth and cashflow with every exchange. These days, all too often, it just flows straight out again – to big utilities or big retailers – and small towns shrivel up. And the planet is heated up further by trucking vegetables across continents. But Ithaca in upstate New York had Paul Glover, who got interested in money when he was working on a radical plan to improve the flow of energy around Los Angeles. He dreamed up the Ithaca hours currency listening to the story of deli dollars (see p 146) on the radio.

His currency works like this. They are printed notes in denominations of 1 hour, 2 hour, half hour, quarter hour and eighth hour notes (hours are worth $10) which are issued into the economy every month in three ways:

• In payment to people who advertise in *Ithaca Money*, the bi-monthly tabloid newspaper which lists the main businesses and services accepting hours – in return for their public backing and for keeping their entries up to date.

• In grants to local charities and non-profit groups: 9.5 per cent of every month's issue is decided by the 'Barter Potluck' – a meeting of anybody interested on the 15th of every month.

• In interest-free loans to local people and business. The biggest local currency loan in the world – the equivalent of over $30,000 – was recently made in Ithaca hours to help the local credit union build new premises.

Ithaca hours were launched in 1991, with the parody slogan on them 'In Ithaca we Trust', and were an immediate success. They are now accepted at over 300 businesses in the town, backed by the mayor and chamber of commerce and accepted at some of the town's banks.

Glover believed that a local currency, because it could only be spent within a 20-mile radius of Ithaca, could at least stem the flood. With its surviving town centre and massive thriving farmers' market, he seems to have been right. Hours have been shown to:

• Give a marketing advantage to local businesses which accept them.

• Provide more income for people on the margins of the economy.

• Substitute local products and services for those flooding in from outside.

• Make the local economy more sustainable, diverse and able to survive recession or inflation.

Glover personally keeps in touch with as many of the users as possible, making sure the currency does not gather anywhere in the system – and if it does, sorting out where it could be spent. It isn't easy launching your own currency and working out how much should be in circulation at any one time without creating the equivalent of inflation. More than 80 other towns across North America have tried the same thing with varying degrees of success.

But even if they haven't all revitalised the local economy – making the best use of local resources and helping local farmers use local markets – the other hours have brought a little colour into small town life.

# DIY money 4

## Time banks and time dollars

*"Market economics values what is scarce – not the real work of society, which is caring, loving, being a citizen, a neighbour and a human being. That work will, I hope, never be so scarce that the market value goes high, so we have to find a way of rewarding contributions to it."*
Edgar Cahn on the thinking behind time dollars

The pioneering law professor Edgar Cahn was concerned about the money system because it only values what is marketable. That can sometimes make it toxic for communities and families, and all those vital human skills that we rely on – to socialise young people, look after the elderly and keep streets safe – get forgotten and disappear (see p 76).

But he has a solution, which he calls 'Co-Production', which sets up a series of reciprocal relationships between professionals, public services and agencies and their clients, using a tax exempt electronic currency called time dollars or time credits, operated through 'time banks'. People earn time by helping out in their neighbourhood, and they spend time when they need help themselves.

Cahn hit on the idea during a prolonged stay in hospital after a heart attack in 1980 – hating the sense of uselessness that he felt there – and persuaded a healthcare foundation to launch six experimental schemes in the USA in 1987. There are now over 100 time banks in the UK, with many more in Japan, China, the USA, Spain and other places. The result is a parallel currency, more a medium of exchange than store of value, that focuses on making neighbourhoods work better – reconnecting people, giving value to people outside the market, and restoring trust. It recognises that almost everybody has something that the community needs – even if it is simply providing a friendly voice over the phone.

Professionals like doctors, teachers or police can't succeed without the active involvement of the community, said Cahn, and time banks provide a way of redefining work so that it includes all this vital but unmarketable work – looking after older people, checking on people coming out of hospital, measuring and rewarding this effort. This is seriously radical money.

Time banks are a solution for our struggling welfare bureaucracies, with increasingly exhausted professionals dealing with increasingly disempowered clients, who are never asked for anything back. They provide a way that both sides can work together so that welfare, health services, education and all the rest actually work. They mean that clients can 'earn' credits also for extra training, sports coaching, computer training. They create a reciprocal relationship that turns welfare beneficiaries into equal partners who are earning by doing the work that society needs.

There is urgent work that needs to be done in society – some of it very simple work like befriending people. We don't have the money to pay for it, but we do have people able to do it, and they must be rewarded so that they can buy the basic necessities of life.

Time banks give back responsibility to people who are regarded as 'the problem' or useless. By so doing, it transforms their lives. Teenage jurors in Washington now cash in their time dollars in return for refurbished computers. Prisoners in Washington earn them by keeping in touch with their children. People with depression earn them by looking after older people. Some innovative projects include:

**Cities**: networks of time banks are now emerging across cities like London (27) and St Louis (11), connecting up projects in a range of different ways so that they support each other (St Louis has linked this into the health system so you can pay doctor's bills in time).

**Schools**: as many as 55 struggling schools in Chicago Albany and London's East End have been pioneering this, paying time credits to pupils as peer tutors, which they cash in for refurbished computers. Academic results go up and bullying goes down.

**After-school clubs:** children in the Slovak city Zilina have organised their own network of six time banks, and contribute to ambitious activities in their after school club.

**Housing:** residents in one public housing complex in Baltimore have been paying part of their rent in time.

**The law:** people in Maryland and California can pay for legal advice in time, paid off sometimes by taking part in demonstrations outside the offices of bad employers.

**Prisons:** women ex-prisoners in San Diego pay for aftercare services in time, paid off by providing support to each other.

**Health:** health centres and health insurance companies are paying time credits to patients for supporting neighbours and even – in Catford – doing basic DIY. Research in Brooklyn shows that people earning time tend to stay healthier.

It costs money to set up time banks – they need a co-ordinator – but the rewards are potentially huge. This resource can plug dwindling budgets and the holes in our pensions. One group of hospitals in Richmond, Virginia, cut the cost of treating asthma patients by more than 70% in two years, by paying them in time to befriend other asthmatics – making sure they were taking their medication, making sure they knew the early warning signs of an attack and knew what to do. Not only did their own symptoms reduce because of the sense of achievement, but the number of asthmatics brought into ER was considerably cut.

Time banks reconnect people and rebuild trust. They may also be very important in the years to some, as policy-makers search desperately for ways to revitalise neighbourhoods.

*Edgar Cahn*
*No More Throwaway People:*
*The co-production imperative*
Essential Books, 2000
ISBN 1893520021

# Green money

## Currencies that make us sustainable

An astonishing three trillion frequent flyer miles issued by airlines over the past ten years are still unspent. If any of their executives doubted whether air miles or nectar points were a kind of money, the airline accountants were quick to explain that they were.

But of course, loyalty points can be more subtle than ordinary money. They are an information system that can use spare capacity to get people to behave in a certain way – and that's just as relevant to cities as it is to companies.

Witness, for example, the extraordinary success of the Brazilian city of Curitiba, which issued points to people for recycling their rubbish – and which were enthusiastically collected by street children handing in litter off the streets. The points could be spent during off-peak times on the buses. The result:

*"The notion of multiple target currencies opens up a new way of thinking in economics."*
Edward de Bono, *The IBM Dollar*

Curitiba is the cleanest city in Latin America, and all paid for by spare public transport capacity.

Rotterdam has launched an even more ambitious project, backed by Rabobank and the transport and waste departments of the city council. It pays electronic points onto a smart card to reward green behaviour – anything from buying eco-label products to recycling. If you buy organic food, or ethical investment products or bicycles, or if you separate your waste and take it to recycling centres, you earn points on your plastic Nu- SpaarPas.

You can spend them on public transport – as in Curitiba – or theatre tickets, or sports training, or going to the zoo, or education, and, eventually, green tourism.

This is similar thinking to that behind the time banks (see p 155). Good neighbourly behaviour and 'green behaviour' take extra time, but nobody notices, nobody rewards it and nobody thanks you. The Nu-SpaarPas means you can reward them with the city's spare capacity – at theatres, in sports centres or on the trams. Thus you can be 'efficient' in a way that simple accountancy with ordinary money never allows.

purists may not like it because it complicates the balance sheet; they sometimes object to the ideas of new kinds of money. Environmental purists may not like it because people should be behaving like this anyway, but Rotterdam is probably a better place to live as a result.

Loyalty points may not change the world, but they do show a way forward that can make all the difference for sustainability, rewarding people for shopping ethically, shopping locally and behaving in a sustainable way. Economic

# Domestic tradable quotas

## Money from the greenhouse effect

*"Money should circulate like rainwater."*
Thornton Wilder

When the greenhouse effect threw up the idea of tradeable carbon emissions permits – now the basis of the endless international climate change negotiations about how much fossil fuels each nation has the right to burn – it provided a whole new possible basis for money.

Imagine, said the policy analyst David Fleming, that those emissions permits are not just credited towards nations, and traded by them, but credited to all of us as individuals and ordinary businesses – rather like wartime ration coupons. In fact it was his childhood experiences with sweet rations that gave him the idea that the permits or coupons could be held on a personal smartcard and either spent or traded, just as nations do.

The idea of 'domestic tradable quotas' (DTQs) was introduced for the first time in an article in *Country Life* in 1996, and immediately caught the attention of the European Commission – only to be developed further with Richard Starkey of the University of Huddersfield. They would, after all, provide a kind of basic income to every individual, as of right (see p 106).

DTQs are intended as a way of involving everyone in reducing our carbon emissions. And in case you don't believe something so elusive could provide the basis for anything that could be bought and sold, it's happening already – and not just in the Chicago exchange that has pioneered carbon trading. Green energy producers on continental Europe are already unbundling the energy from the 'green-ness' – and selling on the green aspect to electricity suppliers in the UK who want to sell green energy but haven't got enough windmills yet to provide it.

The DTQ idea works like this:

- The UK agrees what its annual carbon 'budget' is during international negotiations. (It will reduce over time.)
- The 'carbon units' making up the budget are issued to adults, companies and organisations. All adults get the same allocation free, but organisations and companies have to bid for them at an auction held by the government.
- Every time you buy energy – either electricity, gas or petrol – you have to hand over some of your credits on an electronic smartcard.
- If you need more, you have to buy them from the national exchange. But if you have been frugal or you have invested in energy-saving improvements at home, you can sell yours and make some money – either through ATM machines, over the counter of banks and post offices and energy retailers, or by direct debit arrangements with energy suppliers.

The scheme makes it very clear to people how much fossil fuel can be used in the future. It is also equal. "The instrument gives consumers themselves a central role in the reduction of carbon emissions," says David Fleming. "It does not act over their heads; it involves them. It is therefore transparent: it is clear to consumers how the scheme works, and how prices are set. There is no sense that there is some anonymous government body setting the prices for them. It is the citizens' own scheme; there is a sense of justice."

# The rise and rise of barter

## Swap shops

*"Money is too important to leave to central bankers."*
Milton Friedman

In traditional societies, barter kept the wheels of the economy turning without cash. If you grew carrots, you could swap them for whatever else you really needed. But economists are wary of barter, and despair when an economy collapses so badly – as in the former Soviet Union in the 1990s – that highly complex barter deals re-emerge, like carrots for tyres, for radio batteries, for cabbages, for neckties and so on.

They are right that it is highly inefficient, because you need to have what the other person wants. But barter using new kinds of electronic currency is very efficient, and is on the rise all over the world. Economists barely recognise it, official statisticians ignore it and so it is a phenomenon that is barely studied, but we do know some things about it:

**It's big**: it now covers somewhere between 10% and 20% of world trade, and much more if you include the old-fashioned barter deals – known as countertrade – that are direct swaps. (One of the most famous countertrade deals was responsible for first putting Stolichnaya vodka into Western shops.)

**It can get you out of a hole**: barter is what economists call 'counter-cyclical': when the economy slides into recession, barter goes up, and vice versa – and there is not much around that does that.

**It measures things better**: barter can give value to your stock even if the global currencies think it is valueless. If you were unwise enough to stock up on purple toothpaste, for example, or you have hotel rooms on specific dates or airline seats that are about to expire, or you want to clear your office of last year's computers (and five million perfectly good computers are put into landfill in the UK every year), then using barter currencies can give them value.

Three big barter exchanges dominate the world of barter: Active International, ICON International and Atwood Richards, and their clients include two out of three of the Fortune 500 companies. But local barter for small business is also growing rapidly. Nearly all exchanges issue their own electronic money called trade dollars or trade pounds as a way of facilitating transactions, which – because it can be insured in the USA – is increasingly taking on some of the attributes of hard currency. There are now over 400 business barter exchanges in the USA alone.

Barter is also getting increasingly sophisticated. When your local exchange can't immediately find what they need, they can use an international currency called 'universal' to barter it from elsewhere. The UK arm of the Australian company Bartercard even encourages clients to donate surplus trade pounds to the Metropolitan Police children's charities.

But the key point is this: if the biggest companies in the world – and some of the smallest – can all use DIY currencies, and benefit from them, why can't the rest of us? Economists say these ideas are irrational and primitive, yet most of the most successful companies in the world are doing it. It's time everyone else did too.

*The value of barter worldwide:*

| | |
|---|---|
| *1999* | *$6.9 billion* |
| *2001* | *$7.9 billion* |

*source: IRTA*

Terry L. Neal and Gary K. Eisler
*Barter and the Future of Money*
MasterMedia, 1996
ISBN 1571010610

# The future of money

## A multi-currency world

*"To scatter plenty o'er a smiling land."*
Thomas Gray, *Elegy written in a country churchyard*

If you want a nail in a peculiar shape, or a weird kind of screwdriver, then you can't go wrong in Lordship Lane, Dulwich: it has a plethora of small DIY shops. But they're an endangered species, because a plan to build a Homebase superstore on one of the last remaining bits of green nearby would probably strip Lordship Lane of this speciality. Although the balance sheets of Homebase will show a big boost, locals will have lost something important.

Why don't these aspects of wealth show up in the figures? If money is supposed to reflect people's preferences, why doesn't it reflect the preferences of the locals? International currencies are blind to this kind of wealth: in the end they price out what is small, local and human, and in the end drive out anything except financial services. Currencies don't measure very well: what they miss out gets ignored, then forgotten. Then it disappears.

Different people need different kinds of money, which behave in different ways and value different assets. But we also all need different kinds of money for different aspects of our lives. If we don't get that, some parts of our cities will be rich and some poor, and some parts of our lives will be rich and some poor in the same way.

That's why we need a range of currencies – time banks to underpin the social economy, local currencies to keep money and resources circulating locally, regional currencies to provide low cost finance to small business. And we need a range of experimental currencies based on anything from renewable energy to the value of local vegetables.

Orthodox economists say this whole business of multiple currencies is never going to happen, but it's happening already. There are 9,000 local currencies now in the world, most of them in Latin America. But there are other kinds of new currencies emerging too – from points on pre-paid phone cards to currencies that seek out spare capacity, whether it is for training or social development or local economic renewal. All of that – and the euro circulating as well, even in the UK.

Local currencies can recognise the skills of local people and bring them together with the jobs that need doing. Big currencies can do that on a continent-wide basis, but they sometimes find it hard in communities that are, for whatever reason, running out of cash.

The green economist Richard Douthwaite proposed four currencies inside one nation:

• **An international currency** for trading between nations, keeping the global economy within the trading capacity of the planet.

• **A national-exchange currency** for trading inside a nation, issued interest-free by the central bank, to encourage commercial activity.

• **User-controlled currencies**, like LETS, time banks and others to underpin different aspects of local life.

• **A store-of-value currency**, for saving – for houses and other capital assets, linking your savings to the prosperity of the nation.

But we don't have to wait for the government to organise it all for us. We have assets around us in ourselves, and new currencies like time credits can recognise and value all those wasted aspects of life – old people's time, young people's time, last year's computers – and direct them at the enormous weight of human need that goes unrecognised and unmeasured.

We can do it ourselves, in other words – not by ourselves, but with each other: we can create the basis for the wealth we need.

Richard Douthwaite
*The Ecology of Money*
Schumacher Briefings
Green Books, 1999
ISBN 1870098811

Section VII

# Spiritual money

Is money an expression of spiritual health? Is there another reality behind it that we need to understand? Is there a mysterious way in which the flow of money reflects other kinds of energy? Who knows – but it's another angle on our broadening view of what wealth might mean…

# Does money exist?

## You can't take it with you, after all

*"Every time a child says 'I don't believe in fairies', there is a little fairy somewhere that falls down dead."*
J. M. Barrie, *Peter Pan*

The days when you could store all your worldly wealth under the mattress, or under the floorboards like George Eliot's miser Silas Marner, have not entirely disappeared – though it never was a very good idea. But still, most of our money exists: only in the brief moments we turn a little of it into cash. The rest of the time it is blips on computers, stored in cyberspace.

If you are wealthy and powerful enough, these blips can be almost infinitely elastic. The Cincinnati investment advisor Paul Herrlinger claimed to be bidding for the Minneapolis store chain Dayton-Hudson for $6.8 billion in 1987 – about $6.7 billion more than the assets of his company. In those heady days, when anyone could borrow anything, he was widely believed on Wall Street and Dayton-Hudson shares climbed $10.

After his lawyer tried to head off disaster by explaining that his client was ill, Herrlinger was asked by TV interviewers on his lawn whether the bid was a hoax. "I don't know," he said. "It's no more a hoax than anything else."

When the sceptical financial writer James Grant called his book *Money of the Mind*, this is what he meant. We now live in a strange world, after all, where the loan we get from the bank is considered by both lender and borrower as an asset.

But there are other senses in which money doesn't exist. So often our relationship with money is an expression of what is going on inside our minds rather than an objective process. Like everything else in life, if you cling onto it too tightly, it tends to seep away. If you give it away – as most religions urge us to give away or 'tithe' at least 10% of our income – it often seems to come back (see p 170).

We also know how much the markets depend on belief to give shares value (see p 42). The value of shares or currencies depends on moods, weather patterns and what traders believe will happen. Belief creates wealth; in other words, it keeps the edifice afloat – otherwise we could not trust each other enough to exchange money. Belief creates money; cynicism undermines it.

In this sense, debt is a serious spiritual malaise – poised between having and not having – and close to the word death from which it derives. In this sense also, the importance of money isn't in its substance – at the heart of most currencies these days there is considerable government debt – it is in the energy behind it. Currency comes from the Latin word 'currens': to circulate. That is what has the effect.

When we believe in it, and when we have relationships with each other, then money circulates and wealth grows. In itself, sitting in the bank, it barely exists at all.

"It takes a village to raise a child. It also takes a village to create money," wrote the Buddhist biologist José Reissig. "To be aware of this is to take a crucial step towards making our lives whole. Money cannot exist by itself; it has no value or meaning apart from us. Ultimately, the equation is very simple: we are it."

Deepak Chopra
*Creating Affluence: The A to Z Guide to a Richer Life*
Bantam Press, 1999
ISBN 0593044959

# Giving it all away

## The thrill of philanthropy

A million Americans are each set to inherit $1 million or more in the next 20 years. A terrifying $8,000 billion – the net worth of all Americans over 50 – will be passing from one generation to the next within 30 years or so. This may be a bounteous gift from one generation, but it can also be a frightening burden.

The problem has generated organisations that support people with inherited wealth – including the Funding Network in London, the Money Meaning and Choices Institute in San Francisco, and the Boston-based Impact Project, which actual encourages them to give it away. It was founded by Anne Slepian and Christopher Mogil, who first realised he had inherited a great deal of money in 1978, when his stockbroker's secretary phoned in case he had any questions about his portfolio. "I was haunted

*"He who does not give what he has, will not get what he wants."*
Henry III, who had this painted over the door to the Painted Chamber of the Palace of Westminster

by the question of why I should have this privilege," he wrote. "I wondered whether I was selfish, pampering myself and avoiding my own insecurities about working. At bottom was a fairly simple question: should I give away my wealth?"

Those who took that dramatic step have included Millard Fuller, the founder of Habitat for Humanity, who gave away everything he had earned to persuade his wife to come back to him. Or Procter & Gamble heir Robbie Gamble. Or Ben Cohen, of Ben & Jerry's ice cream, who tries to give away as much as he spends. In 1986 he gave away $500,000 of stock to launch the Ben & Jerry's Foundation.

Even the TV mogul Ted Turner gave away $1 billion to UN projects. Domino Pizza founder

Thomas Monaghan sold the company for a similar amount and gave it away, after reading C S Lewis's book *Mere Christianity*. Another was James Rouse, the inventor of the shopping mall and 'festival marketplace'.

"I was cared for by a black woman named Gussie from the South Side of Chicago," wrote Edorah Frazer, a teacher who gave away $450,000 – 75% of her inheritance – in her 20s. "She worked for my family until I was in high school. I always noticed that her clothes were different and that she rode the bus while we drove. My first awareness of class differences came from her presence in our household."

Edorah gave away her wealth in piles of share certificates two days before Christmas. "Outside it was raining, and across the street I saw two Salvation Army men with a bucket ringing a bell. The rain was falling on me and I started to cry. It felt really clean, so simple. Although I was happy, I thought: I'm lonely. I wish I had done this with someone. Then immediately I thought: 'No, it's good that I did it alone, because it is a very individual act'. Ultimately I am alone in this decision. It's my story. I crossed the street, took out all the money in my wallet and put it into the Salvation Army bucket."

Giving it away is a traditional theme in all religions, many of which encourage their members to give away at least 10% of what they earn as a tithe. Some say that this kind of giving can release some of the energy about money, and that – if you start doing so – it can also flow back to you more freely. This is of course completely illogical economically, but then so are a lot of things that work.

The traditional Christian view is that belongings should only lie on your shoulders like a light cloak, which can be thrown aside. Unfortunately, the cloak became an iron cage, said the pioneer sociologist Max Weber. That's why giving money away can, paradoxically, make you wealthier.

Christopher Mogil and Anne Slepian
*We Gave Away a Fortune*
New Society, 1992
ISBN 0865712212

# Downshifting

## Voluntary simplicity

*"Life is frittered away by detail ... simplify, simplify."*
Henry David Thoreau, *Walden*

The management guru Charles Handy tells a story about meeting an attractive girl at a party, hearing that she is a freelance TV scriptwriter, but then discovering that she has actually only ever sold one script. "But what do you do for money?" he asks. "Oh, for money I pack eggs on Sundays."

The point he was making was that people are increasingly defining themselves, not by their jobs, but by their dreams – or something else. And for many people, dreams do not include working fingers to the bone to earn more money than the neighbours. They might be about earning deliberately just enough to live where they want to.

In many ways, apparently wealthy societies display a hidden misery and quiet desperation. "People are very empty and they are looking for much deeper passions in life than those provided through material accumulation or through vicarious association with status symbols and people who represent them," said the American futurist Gerald Celente. The phenomenon of downshifting has emerged as a result.

The mere existence of 'downshifters' is another nail in the coffin of economic theories which suppose that we all, always, seek to maximise our income. It is also a testimony to growing resistance to the rat-race. Even at the height of the boom in the richest country in the world – the USA – there were 7,000 bankruptcies an hour during working hours, and people were guzzling anti-depressants at an alarming rate.

There have always been people like Henry David Thoreau or Tom and Barbra Good from *The Good Life*, but the latest generation of downshifters were launched by Duane Elgin, the American author of the influential book *Voluntary Simplicity*. He defined it as "the deliberate choice to live with less in the belief that more of life will be returned to us in the process".

Downshifting by the 1990s was about being less busy, taking more time, and trying to get off the treadmill to live a bit more authentically – which by then usually meant making relationships more central in our lives. This simple definition of downshifting would mean that up to a quarter of the British and US population are 'downshifters' in one sense or another.

But of all the downshifters, the most fanatical was Amy Dacyczyn. She and her husband Jim had both been working for 20 years – she as a graphic designer, he in the US Navy – but had amassed savings of just $1,500. So they set about the task of not spending money with enormous imagination and enthusiasm. After seven years, they had saved $49,000 from Jim's salary and bought a farmhouse in Maine. But that wasn't the end. Amy put her discoveries into a newsletter called *The Tightwad Gazette*, so that everybody else could benefit from her ideas, which include:

- Avoid make-up when nobody is coming to visit.
- When you boil the kettle, pour the excess into a thermos so that you won't have to waste energy re-boiling it later.
- Eke out your margarine with skimmed milk.

By the mid-1990s, she had made such a success of *The Tightwad Gazette* that she was ironically rich enough to retire. When she was first included in *Parade* magazine in 1990, she received 44 feet of mail. Two other organisations that have done more than most to encourage simpler living are:

**The New Road Map Foundation**, the Seattle-based thinktank founded by Joe Dominguez and Vicky Rubin, co-authors of the bestseller *Your Money or your Life*, which set out how to live a simpler, independent life; the book also made a fleeting appearance in the film *American Beauty* (www.newroadmap.org).

**Adbusters**, the Vancouver-based campaign against consumer advertising and mind control – producing the most extraordinary posters, designed by advertising executives working at night (www.adbusters.org).

These and others have together built one of the most powerful movements in the world, a critique of the way money can undermine 'real wealth', the spiritual rage that underpins the anti-globalisation campaign, and a step-by-step guide to doing something about it in your own life – to have life more abundantly.

*Number of Europeans deliberately taking a*
*cut in salary or hours: 12 million.*
*Number opting out of the rat race*
*completely: 2 million.*

Source: Datamonitor, 2003

Polly Ghazi
*The 24-hour Family: A Parents' Guide to the*
*Work-life Balance*
Women's Press, 2003
ISBN 0704347636

# Ethical consumption

## Vigilantes in the supermarket aisles

*"To live means to buy, to buy means to have power, to have power means to have duties."*
National Consumer League motto, 19th century

The idea that people would put their money towards the most ethical buy rather than the cheapest was anathema to free marketeers, yet the success of the *Green Consumer Guide* by John Elkington and Julia Hailes (1988) showed just how much scope there was. When supermarkets realised that up to 40% of their customers would pay more for 'ethical' products – green, organic or fair trade – they hurried to oblige.

The whole phenomenon began with the boycott of South African products under apartheid, and reached a crescendo with the Marine Stewardship Council (conserving fish), the Forest Stewardship Council (sustainable wood) and the Ethical Trading Initiative (tackling sweatshops). The rise of organic food, dolphin-friendly tuna, recycled paper, fair-trade coffee and energy-saving lightbulbs are testament to the power of the ethical consumer.

But consumerism can only go so far by itself. It can punish corporations – as it punished Esso after their efforts to undermine the Kyoto agreement. It can occasionally lead to 'fairer' products on the shelves, but people can still only choose the best on offer. It leaves the basic structures, the bogus advertising and the fuel-consuming out-of-town shopping centres, intact. Even so, there have been notable successes:

- Lead-free petrol is now the market leader.
- Organic food consumption is growing at the rate of 25% a year in the UK. Taken together with fair-trade food, the market was up by over a quarter between 2001 and 2002.

• 'Green' mortgages grew by more than 50% in 2002 alone.

• Free-range eggs are increasingly popular, though the market for eggs is dropping generally.

• Dolphin-friendly tuna is almost the only kind in the UK shops.

The UK ethical market is now worth about £6.8 billion a year, and growing steadily – not 176 of a global market worth about £350 billion. Ethical consumerism can also lead to more sophisticated ideas, such as:

**Consumer co-ops**: like Tokyo's Seikatsu Club, begun by a small group of housewives in 1965 to bring better quality milk into the city in bulk. Organised at street level, the club reached a membership of six figures, running its own bakery and a series of farms. They even got members elected to local government under the slogan 'political reform from the kitchen'.

**Community-supported agriculture**, which began in the USA, whereby households pay a subscription to local farmers to provide them with regular fresh local produce. This provides a guaranteed income to the farmer when they need it most: before they can sell their harvest.

**Slow food**: the Slow Food movement was the brainchild of Carlo Petrini, launched in response to a McDonald's opening in Rome's Piazza di Spagna in 1986. From their headquarters in Bra in Piedmont, at the foot of the Alps – a region known for its truffles and red wine – they have since taken up the cause of long-tailed sheep of Laticauda, Siennese pigs, Vesuvian apricots and many other half-forgotten foods.

# Ethical investment

## Money as morality

In some ways the best ethical purchase – the one that challenges traditional market assumptions the most – is to invest ethically: not where you get the highest returns, but where you most change the world for the better.

The idea that you had to get the best returns, regardless of morality – which many charity trustees still believe – always was ridiculous. These so-called responsibilities forced anti-smoking organisations to invest in tobacco firms, and peace campaigners to invest in arms manufacturers. Even the Church of England – whose Church Commissioners were endlessly repeating that they were legally obliged to invest for the highest returns – turned out to be investing in the Playboy Channel.

*"What is your money doing tonight?"*
The newsletter of the Self-Help Association for a Regional Economy in Great Barrington, Massachusetts

More people on both sides of the Atlantic are thinking more carefully about their wealth, making sure it is invested to make the world a better place – or at least no worse. A group of New England Methodists set the ball rolling in 1971 during the Vietnam War by setting up the Pax World mutual fund, which did not invest in weapons. Now it's worth $9 billion.

In the UK, ethical investment began formally in 1984 with Friends Provident. Their ethical unit trust was known in the City as the 'Brazil Fund' because it was considered a little 'nutty', but in its first year it was in the top ten performers and now there is £3.5 billion invested ethically in Britain.

Ethical investment came of age over the past few years with the launch of the FTSE4Good Index of

Ethical Stock, and its US counterpart, the Dow Jones Sustainable Indexes. It has also benefited by new regulations that require investment funds to make a statement of their ethical position, if any – which has led a number of funds to be more ethical than before. (There are now 50 strictly ethical funds.)

But one of the peculiarities of the ethical investment world is that it can mean a range of different techniques, including:

**Best of sector investment** (like FTSE4Good), which means picking the best-behaving company in each sector and investing accordingly. That could mean investing in companies that are really not ethical by any stretch of the imagination, including big oil companies – because it depends entirely on the stage of development in the rest of the sector.

**Positive ethical investment**, that seeks out genuinely ethical companies to invest in.

**Ethical engagement**, which means precisely the reverse – choosing companies that are not ethical enough and using the share-holding to put pressure on them.

Ethical investment is getting political in its own right. After all, is best-of-sector investing really ethical? Some companies that receive ethical investment may behave well within certain set parameters – they tick the right boxes in how they treat their staff, for example – but their basic product is sometimes still unsustainable. Oil companies, for example. Or British Nuclear Fuels. In 2001, the Dow Jones Sustainable Index dropped 46 companies (including Disney), but FTSE4Good didn't drop any.

The result is that the vast majority of UK ethical funds invest in just a few stocks (they include Abbey National and Vodafone) – not exactly ethical, just avoiding such things as tobacco and arms. Ethical investment needs to go further, and the next stage of the campaign is going to include:

**More shareholder engagement**: when chief executives earn millions undeservedly then it is a failure of shareholders to exert pressure.

**More ethical share issues**: to raise money for ethical projects. The Ethical Property Company managed to raise £4.2 million in 2002 in a share issue to open more office space for 'social change' organisations.

**More ethical banks:** Triodos Bank now has branches in four European countries, lending only to ethical projects and businesses. The Aston Reinvestment Trust and the London Rebuilding Society funnel investment money where it is needed the most, and more big banks – like the Co-operative Bank – are putting ethics at the heart of everything they do.

**More local bond issues:** local government is not allowed to issue bonds to raise their own finance in the UK – that's why they are so pathetically dependent on central government. But in the USA, local bonds for housing finance are so safe that they are the key element in most people's pensions.

*Ethical investment funds in the UK:*

| | |
|---|---|
| *1989* | *£199m* |
| *1995* | *£792m* |
| *1999* | *£2,447m* |
| *2002* | *£4,025m* |

# Greed therapy

## The basis of the problem

It's an old truism that there is enough on the planet for everyone's need but not for everyone's greed. But it is extremely difficult to tell the two apart in practice, because greed is often simply the expression of people's fear that their needs won't be met.

The truth is that money represents considerably more than whatever is written on it. For most of us, it is linked in strange subconscious tangles with love, security, freedom, power and self-worth. This is at least partly because we are never taught – or at least never fully believe – that money is just a means to an end, and it isn't a means to every end either.

The results of greed and its excesses are all around us. American parents have recently been buying their children quarter-sized fully operational Range Rovers ($18,500) for Christmas, or life-sized reproductions of Darth Vader ($5,000), or paying $250,000 for bar-mitzvahs in Manhattan.

But greed may not be quite what it seems. It isn't quite sane to need more and more and more, and the mega-rich are often those who have an overwhelming fear of poverty that forces them to carry on pushing when any normal human being would sit back and enjoy life. The result is that "money and time are the heaviest burdens of life," according to Samuel Johnson, "and the unhappiest of all mortals are those who have more of either than they know how to use."

> *"A somewhat disgusting morbidity, one of the semi-criminal, semi-pathological propensities which one hands over with a shudder to the specialists in mental disease."*
> J. M. Keynes on the love of money

That is why a new kind of therapy has begun to emerge which helps people tackle their problems with money. Sometimes that relates to their greed – though calling yourself a 'greed therapist' doesn't encourage customers – but it can also help people confront their money neuroses and the way it divides them from others.

Often this means confronting the most basic beliefs. Even the idea that money means security in old age isn't entirely true: older people who are most secure are not necessarily those who are financially independent; they are those who can rely on being part of a supportive family and neighbourhood (see p 76).

In most couples for example, one will play the role of the hoarder and one the role of the spender – sometimes playing different roles in different relationships. Often they actually secretly admire the other's ability to hoard or to spend – but daren't admit it, in case it encourages them to go wild or become more miserly.

The key point is that money isn't actually love or security at all. It's just money. And if your clients still don't get it, you can always campaign for one new idea from radical economists – a 70% 'Additional Consumption Tax' on outrageous luxuries like the mini Range Rover.

**If you give more, focus on what you have and build your self-esteem, you won't be so obsessive about money either – and maybe that is the beginning of real wealth.**

Dorothy Rowe
*The Real Meaning of Money*
HarperCollins, 1997
ISBN 0006381227

# Alchemy

## The lure of the philosopher's stone

*"The only thing money cannot buy is meaning."*
Jacob Needleman

The 13th-century pioneer of chemistry, Roger Bacon, explained that alchemy "teaches us how to make the noble metals and colours and many other things better and more copiously by art than they can be made by nature." It is more important than other sciences, he went on, "since it produces most useful products, giving not only the monies and other expenses of the state, but the wherewithal to prolong life."

At its best, alchemy was about change – about changing and perfecting people as much as changing metals. It was about using what we have to create wealth, in its broadest sense. As the Middle Ages went by, alchemy also attracted a radical protestant edge to it. Alchemists like the mysterious Paracelsus – wandering round Europe

in a coloured coat which he never washed – were the inspiration behind a protestant revolution against the old order of authority and control.

They threatened the old certainties of medicine and politics with their dreams of a 'chemical revolution' which would restore humanity, attacking monopolies and putting power and

medical knowledge in the hands of ordinary people. And now, five centuries on, there is a new kind of alchemy emerging, working out how to take those ordinary assets we have around us – skills, care, abilities, forgotten resources that the narrow economy doesn't recognise – and using them to enhance life. This is a demonstration, at every level of society, that by working together we can all create the equivalent of gold.

It is another Protestant revolution of a kind, which says that the solution to the problem isn't to hand over more power to the priests (the bankers) to create money for us, still less to the king (the government) to do it – but to find ways that we can create the money we need ourselves. It also recognises that for the word 'wealth' to mean anything at all, it is going to have to go a long way beyond mere money.

www.levity.com/alchemy

# Conclusion

*"Once we allow ourselves to be disobedient to the test of an accountant's profit, we have begun to change our civilisation."*
John Maynard Keynes, 1933

*"Our deepest fear is not that we are powerless. Our deepest fear is that we are powerful beyond measure."*
Nelson Mandela, 1994

So what are we to make of it all? If you can sum up the various messages of this Little Book – and money covers the whole of human life, after all – they probably amount to the following.

1. There is a fundamental moral problem about the way we use money: it isn't immoral, but it is amoral – it values unimportant things (McDonald franchises, foreign exchange, hedge funds) highly, and important things (families, communities, nurses) little.

2. Because of this, it tends to drive out what's good in society, and what's vital for our lives. Big currencies drive out variety, diversity and creativity – leaving just money behind. And if you don't believe me, look at Jersey.

3. Money seems to be running out – at least for the vital things in life – because useless but lucrative investments where money breeds on money suck it all up, and we find that the money for real things gets whittled away.

In other words, the conclusion is the same as Ruskin's: there is no wealth but life. But the danger is becoming clearer every year. People who want to produce books or grow barley or sell food now have to do so through the gaps, and with the crumbs that are the by-products of speculation, of the financial roundabout that booms above them and produces nothing real. One day, it may be impossible.

It is a very practical problem, but it is also primarily a moral one – one that no amount of legislation can solve. People in every age have confused money with real value, and they probably always will – but can we teach people to beware of the confusion and point them towards its consequences?

It is important that we understand our own responsibility towards money. The 'original sin' of interest may be laying waste to the environment because it demands such high growth and high returns, but most of us are also implicated in it with our savings, our mortgages and our pensions.

Money is not as good a measuring system as it claims to be. It measures well what the financial system and the global traders believe is important, but extremely badly what is important to ordinary people. When it comes to the fundamentals of life, it is practically blind.

What can be done about it? We can persuade the government to issue more money interest-free, rather than letting banks create it all. We can make sure, either by laws or taxes, that the full costs of enterprises are reflected in prices, that subsidies for unsustainable activities end and the polluters pay for their damage. We can find ways to make money circulate better in local communities without seeping out to middlemen and distant corporations. We can try to make sure that nobody gets paid – for the sake of argument – more than a hundred times more than anyone else. It doesn't sound much, does it?

We should beware of catch-all solutions that are supposed to solve everything, whether they are land tax or monetary reform. There may be a place for a measure of both, but they will never change the world by themselves. The law of unintended consequences hangs heavy over single solutions, and especially over any idea that we ought to centralise the money supply so that only the government or their chosen representatives are allowed to create it.

Centralisation and monopoly have always tended

towards tyranny and monoculture, and that is the problem with money too.

One approach to the money problem is to re-introduce diversity. Big currencies, big global systems tend towards monoculture; they drive out anything that's different, whether they are other languages, other cultures or other species. An economy that is human and real is one with a diversity of measuring systems, and that means a diversity of kinds of money – not neatly segregated by national boundaries, but overlapping.

That's why I believe the future of money lies in multiple currencies, to underpin different aspects of our lives. The US dollar circulates throughout most of the world – in fact a third of dollar bills in circulation are outside the USA – just as the euro is beginning to circulate in Britain. But we need more: local currencies, green currencies, small business currencies, loyalty currencies, time currencies, city currencies, babysitting currencies – to give ordinary people and places that don't quite fit into the shiny new world of globalisation what they need to maintain life.

The future of money is that we all create it,

enough for what we need. Greed creates inflation, but a diversity of currencies will allow us to bypass such problems.

There are also things we can do as individuals to tackle the money system at its most corrupt, and they are all to do with making wealth, money, places and life real and human again:

### Real, human wealth

We may not be able to turn money values on their heads, at least by ourselves. But we can buy and invest according to what is most human. We can buy what is made locally, made by craftspeople and small producers, or invest in projects that will help such people, not where the financial experts, the marketeers or the markets urge us to invest. We can buy fair-trade goods direct from the communities that make them. We can use our intuition, and inform ourselves about which global brands are owned by which global monsters, and withdraw our support from companies that lay waste to the earth and its inhabitants. We have a small vote in the global marketplace – our buying power – and we should use it.

## Real, human places

We have choice about what kind of places our high streets and towns become, and we can use our time and money accordingly. We can shun fast food and mega-malls, and take our custom whenever we can to shops and restaurants that are owned locally. (And when we cannot avoid fast food and modern machine systems, we can at least chat to the poor de-humanised staff behind the counters.) When we use supermarkets, we can demand that they have a choice of fruit and vegetables from the country in which they are operating.

## Real, human money

We may not be able to stop the dematerialisation of money, but then that isn't really the point. We can help the spread of diverse new kinds of money to underpin a diverse world. We can innovate with the points systems of big corporations, use them in ways that weren't intended – trading nectar points or donating them to charity. We can use local currencies and, where they are not available, we can barter or give things away. We can join our local time bank, and join any local system that supports and funds local food or local production.

## Real, human life

Again, we can't stand up by ourselves against the weight of the system, but we can – just by working on our own lives – hold out against it, and maybe by example encourage others to do so. We can encourage simplicity and creativity. We can put our relationships and our creative lives a little higher in our list of priorities. We can give more, and sometimes maybe even accept more in return. We can do things for free, we can surprise people by our semi-independence from the financial world. We can find and celebrate the inner wealth in people that the market sidelines – and in ourselves.

These are all hard to do, for me as much as for everybody else. We may not transform the financial system, but we will probably feel 'wealthier' as a result.

David Boyle
Crystal Palace
May 2003

# Internet resources

## Metal money

British Museum www.thebritishmuseum.ac.uk/worldofmoney

Bank of England www.bankofengland.co.uk

Roy Davies, money history www.ex.ac.uk/~RDavies/arian/money.html

Democracy and the IMF www.undp.org/hdr2002

E-gold www.egold.com

Federal Reserve www.federalreserve.gov

IMF reform www.halifaxinitiative.org

World Bank reform www.brettonwoodsproject.org

## Information money

Alaska Permanent Fund www.apfc.org

Consult Hyperion (e-cash) www.hyperion.co.uk

GRAIN (biodiversity) www.grain.org

Financial scandals www.ex.ac.uk/~RDavies/arian/scandals/

Institute for Policy Study www.ips.dc.org

Internat. Forum Globalisation www.ifg.org

Global Policy Forum www.globalpolicy.org

Bernard Lietaer www.transaction.net/money/bio/lietaer.html

New Internationalist www.oneworld.org/ni

Multinational Monitor www.essential.org

Plugging the Leaks project www.pluggingtheleaks.org

World Trade Organisation www.wto.org

Yes! (positive futures) www.yesmagazine.org

## Measuring money

Bowling Alone (social capital) www.bowlingalone.com

Environmental indicators www.sustainablemeasures.com

Amitai Etzioni (social capital)www .amitai-notes.com

ISEA (social auditing) www .accountability.org.uk

Richard Layard (happiness) cep.lse.ac.uk

New Economics Foundation www.neweconomics.org

Andrew Oswald (happiness) www.oswald.co.uk

Redefining Progress www.rprogress.org

Securities & Exchange Cssn www.sec.gov

Tyranny of Numbers www.tyrannyofnumbers.co.uk

## Debt money

Citizens Income www.citizensincome.org

Forum for Stable Currencies www.intraforum.net/money

Grameen Bank www.grameen-info.org

Institute for Fiscal Studies www.ifs.org.uk

Inst. for Local Self-Reliance www.ilsr.org

Jubilee Debt Campaign www.jubileedebtcampaign.org.uk

Jubilee Research www.jubileeplus.org

Micro-credit virtual library www.gdrc.org/icm/

Mortgages www.mortgagesexposed.com

Odious Debts www.odiousdebts.org

Pensions Ombudsman www.pensions-ombudsman.org.uk

Prosperity UK www.prosperityuk.com

Social Credit Secretariat www.douglassocialcredit.com

## Mad money

Corporate Predators www.corporatepredators.com
Ecologist magazine www.theecologist.org
Charles MacKay (delusions)
www.econlib.org/library/Mackay/macExtoc.html
Money Laundering Alert www.moneylaundering.com
Post Autistic Economics www.paecon.net
Tobin Tax www.ceedweb.org

## DIY money

Barataria (currency consulting) www.barataria.org
Barter www.irta.com
Community money in the south ccdev.lets.net
Complementary currencies www.transaction.net
Domestic tradable quotes www.dtqs.org
Fair Shares (time banks) www.fairshares.org
Funny Money www.funny-money.co.uk
Ithaca Hours www.ithacahours.org
Letslink Scotland www.letslinkscotland.org.uk
LETSystems www.gmlets.u-net.com
Michael Linton www.openmoney.org
London Time Bank www.londontimebank.org.uk
Nu-SpaarPas www.nuspaarpas.nl
E. F. Schumacher Society www.schumachersociety.org
Time Banks UK www.timebanks.co.uk
Time dollars www.timedollar.org

## Spiritual money

Adbusters www.adbusters.org
Breakthrough Centre www.lifeshift.co.uk
Co-Op America (consumer) www.coopamerica.org
Co-operative Bank www.co-operativebank.co.uk
EIRIS (ethical investment) www.eiris.org
Ethical Performance www.ethicalperformance.com
Napoleon Hill www.naphill.org
Resurgence www.resurgence.org
Sweatshops www.sweatshopwatch.org
Triodos Bank www.triodos.co.uk

## Some other helpful web addresses:

## Ethical Investment

Charcol Holden-Meehan (financial services)
www.holden-meehan.co.uk
Rathbones (stockbrokers) www.rathbones.com
London Rebuilding Society
www.londonrebuilding.com
Aston Re-investment Trust www.reinvest.co.uk
The Funding Network (philanthropy)
www.thefundingnetwork.org.uk
Triodos Bank www.triodos.co.uk

# The Little Earth Book

'Only dead fish float with the current;
live fish swim against it'.

By James Bruges

Now in its third edition, this is as engrossing and provocative as ever, and continues to highlight the perilously fragile state of our planet. Little Earth makes the perfect companion to Little Food, so why not order a copy of each to make sure you understand just how much is at stake in our world today.

You can find out more about both these titles by visiting our website www.fragile-earth.com

"The Little Earth Book is different. And instructive. And even fun!"

Jonathan Porritt,
Forum for the Future

www.fragile-earth.com

# The Little Food Book

An explosive account of the food we eat today

by Craig Sams

The Little Earth Book has proved immensely popular. And because we think some of the issues raised are so important, we've published another book – **The Little Food Book.**

It tackles the issues on our own plates: genetic modification, the food chain, farming subsidies, obesity and many others – all affecting the food we eat. Who controls what we eat? What happens to it before it gets to us?

This tough little book reveals how our food affects not just our health but the well-being of the whole planet.

Easy-to-read yet hugely informative and stimulating.

"This is a really big little book. Craig Sams knows his subject and his warnings about the food we eat are based on scrupulous evidence."

Jonathan Dimbleby, President of the Soil Association

www.fragile-earth.com

# SPECIAL PLACES TO STAY SERIES

"...takes the hard work out of choosing just the right place for a weekend away."

The Daily Telegraph

Alastair Sawday also publishes the much-loved travel guide series – **Special Places to Stay.** If you are serious about travelling well – meeting interesting people, eating good regional food, avoiding chain hotels and burger-bars, etc – then you'd love these remarkable books. What's more, you'll probably also eat a lot of organic food and be 'pumping' your holiday money into the rural economy. Visit our website at www.specialplacestostay.com

www.specialplacestostay.com

# Biography

David Boyle first became interested in money when he was an environment journalist, frustrated at the way that it made things either possible or impossible - and first came across local currencies in New Zealand in 1991, when 'green dollars' were taking off there. Since then, he has written widely about money from a green and ethical perspective, and spoken about new kinds of money to audiences ranging from European bankers to e-cash experts.

His books *Funny Money* (1999), *Why London Needs its own Currency* (2000), *Virtual Currencies* (2001) and *The Money Changers* (2002) have all reflected this interest in changing the way the system works. He was also instrumental in bringing the idea of time banks to the UK.

He is an associate of the New Economics Foundation, and editor of their newspaper *Radical Economics*. He has been editor also of *Town & Country Planning* and *Liberal Democrat News* and has written and broadcast widely on a range of subjects including cities, economics and the future. He is the author of *The Tyranny of Numbers* (2001), *The Sum of Our Discontent* (2002) and *Authenticity: Brands, Fakes, Spin and the Lust for Real Life* (2003).